KEITH MOON
STOLE MY LIPSTICK

KEITH MOON STOLE MY LIPSTICK

THE SWINGING '60S, THE GLAM '70S AND ME

JUDITH WILLS

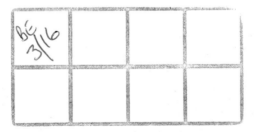

Cover image: iStock

First published by UKA Press, 2008
New edition published by The History Press, 2016

The History Press
The Mill, Brimscombe Port
Stroud, Gloucestershire, GL5 2QG
www.thehistorypress.co.uk

British Library Cataloguing in Publication Data.
A catalogue record for this book is available from the British
Library.

ISBN 978 0 7509 6609 2

Typesetting and origination by The History Press
Printed in Great Britain

PRAISE FOR KEITH MOON STOLE MY LIPSTICK

'Evocative', 'Funny', 'Touching', 'Shocking', 'Delightful', 'An elegy to lost innocence'.

'Enjoyed every minute of the book – didn't we all have charmed lives? It was a delightful read from the perspective of an innocent in the '60s/'70s lion's den – one of the many strengths in the story.'
Tony Prince, ex-Radio Luxembourg DJ,
founder DMC

'A funny, poignant, delightful memoir. Wills is never less than frank about the stars she meets in her eight frantic years in London on a pop magazine.'
Phillipa May, leisure editor,
Hereford Times

'It hits the spot – sparks off so many memories for me ... compelling.'
Nick Owen, BBC presenter,
Midlands Today

'It's compulsive reading; well written and humorous. I empathised with the author and cared about what happened to her. It beautifully captures what it must have been like to be a young person in the hip, happening times of the late '60s and '70s. Titbits about the celebs are very interesting and often funny. I love it.

Sarah MacPherson, chartered psychologist, London

'If you're looking for a gift for the music fan in your life, consider this great, funny new book.'

wnew.com

'I honestly couldn't put it down!'

Chris McLoughlin, freelance health editor

'I found it fascinating to read – I went through lots of emotions. Laughter at times, sadness, sometimes shock. I couldn't move until I had finished it.'

Nesta Parsons, retired factory manager, housewife and mother

'An enjoyable, nostalgic and evocative read,
whether or not you are of an age to remember
the legend of the title himself. I found the
author's own story just as fascinating as
the anecdotal tales of the celebrities she
encounters. I particularly like the easy,
accessible style of writing. Sequel please!'

Coral Jane, artist

'I really enjoyed it! It was good to have the
culture of that era brought to life, especially as
the author is an 'ordinary' person.'

Sarah Giles, freelance editor

'What a fantastic book this is – I really couldn't
put it down!! It has a lovely style.

I found myself trying to pre-empt the
wonderfully evocative descriptions (who would
the boy with funny teeth dancing round the
office turn out to be?!).

I saw the '70s as a schoolboy but lived them
again through the book from a totally different
perspective.'

*Simon Nicholls, Courtyard Theatre,
Hereford*

'Because the author tells her story so very well, I often forgot I was reading someone's memoirs and read it like a novel – it's charming.'

Lara Hale, freelance journalist

'This is a rattling good tale but with an underlying deeper, sadder story of a driving determination to succeed against the odds.

I found it a page turner, and I think young people will love it too.'

Ann McDonnell, retired
behavioural therapist

'It's very readable – once you start you want to keep on. It's nice and light but with some poignant moments too. Just all the famous people she knew is enough to get you hooked. It's very funny, too.'

Julia Smith, freelance publicist

Contents

Introduction

An Inauspicious Beginning

While California had its 'summer of love', Britain was better – far, far better. We were swinging to The Beatles' 'All You Need is Love', Procol Harum's 'Whiter Shade of Pale' and the Stones' 'Let's Spend the Night Together'. We had The Who, Twiggy, Carnaby Street, Biba and Mary Quant, Radio Caroline. We had it all. London, England – this was the only place to be as the celebrity culture began to explode.

And then there was me. A star-struck 17-year-old country bumpkin complete with country bumpkin accent, country bumpkin clothes and country bumpkin attitude. Graduate of the world-famous Oxford College of Technology with two A levels and a couple of dubious secretarial skills. Shy, frightened of almost everything, ignorant of the ways of London, the media, music and sophisticates in general, and completely devoid of self-confidence.

Despite this distinct lack of any obvious potential as a member of the beautiful people club or even the lower echelons of the pop or media worlds, I moved to London anyway, got a break and was soon living a life every bored secretary, shift worker, schoolgirl or pop music fan could only dream about (myself included). A life filled daily with all the fabulousness that was the music, movie and press scene of the late '60s and through the '70s. And I got paid for it. And I lived to tell the story.

Yes, I really was there. I spent several crazy years immersed in the world of popstars, musicians, movies, TV, theatre, actors and every kind of celebrity you could imagine. I was there, soon after the start of the cult of celebrity in all its forms. I was there at the start of mass hysteria for boy bands (think The Monkees, The Osmonds, Jackson Five, Bay City Rollers). Think of the biggest names the world of post-war music has ever produced – The Beatles, The Doors, The Stones, The Who, Queen – and I was there seeing it all, seeing them, first-hand. From Jimi Hendrix and Joan Baez through to Slade and Marc Bolan, from the last breaths of festival hippiedom through to glamrock, bubblegum and the start of punk, I was there.

Veering uncertainly between taking it all for granted, wondering what I'd landed myself into, panicking about how soon I'd get caught out as a useless imposter hick, and pinching myself hard to prove I really was not dreaming.

I lived in it and through it, with it and, I suppose, for it – observing, dipping in, enthralled, occasionally objective. My shyness often worked for me but just as often, my youth and stupidity got me into minor scrapes and major difficulties. Although sometimes it was just like I'd imagined – when I'd dreamed of being a pop writer during several depressing early teenage years through which my pop and TV heroes had sustained me – at other times it was nowhere near. There were bad bits: big bad bits. Some of it wasn't so much fab as just plain weird.

Decades later I'm just an ordinary wife, mum and writer – back in the country with few links to that world apart from my unique bag of memories that have provided a source of great fun, wonder and supper party moments for my circle of friends. 'You really met Freddie Mercury/Paul McCartney/Jim Morrison/Mr Spock/Robert Redford ...' etc., etc., etc. And before I know it, I'm off on one – another story comes intact and fresh as ever, out of a brain that hasn't recalled it for years.

How did I manage all this? Well, first get yourself an older sister who works as a secretary at a London publishing company and who notices there's a job going on another magazine in the same company, as editor's secretary. Make sure sister tells you about it. Apply for an interview. The rest is easy. Ish. The biggest blag of all time and not as difficult to achieve as you might imagine. Well, if I could do it anyone could.

One week I was sitting in the wilds of Oxfordshire with no job, the next I was working for the 'original and best' pop magazine that I'd spent the past five years avidly reading, and whose colour photos were taped to my bedroom walls. I became friendly – or at least, on hugging terms – with many of the biggest names of the '70s as well as relics from the '60s and megastars of future years when they were still the equivalent of X-Factor hopefuls or, in some cases, babes in arms. I dated a few of them as well. Occasionally I turned down some very famous people while, sadly, several stars I fluttered my false eyelashes at chose to ignore the challenge.

So who would blame me on the days I did pinch myself – how many people wake up on a Monday morning and feel nothing but pit-of-the-stomach excitement at the thought of going to work? How many people can say they have danced with David Bowie, sung with Freddie Mercury, smoked a joint with Jim Morrison, been read *The Book of Mormon* by an Osmond and, of course, had their lipstick stolen by Keith Moon? And there was more; plenty more.

So if you want to know the mad, fab and sometimes bad detail – grab a drink, and let's be off.

one

Hot Town

1967

Elvis married Priscilla in May. Evel Knievel has jumped over sixteen cars on his motorbike. The Beatles have a new album out – *Sgt. Pepper's Lonely Hearts Club Band*. The single 'San Francisco (Be Sure to Wear Some Flowers in Your Hair)' by Scott McKenzie has just popped into the charts. And Keith Richards has been sentenced to a year in jail for possessing illegal drugs.

Drip, drip drip. Drip, drip drip.

It's July. I'm in bed, half asleep. It may be the summer of love in San Francisco but here in London it's wet. My head's wet, anyway. No – it's not rain. The ceiling's leaking.

Monday morning; my first morning in my very first bedsit. But this isn't the start I'd planned. I'd wanted the rhythm of music to wake me up – The Beatles' 'All You Need is Love', say, or 'Pictures of Lily', the new single from The Who – not the damp annoying beat of dripping water. Never mind, saves washing hair.

(Did I say bedsit? Not much of a bedsit – a tiny single bedroom in someone else's apartment with use of their K and B (kitchen and bathroom). The leaseholder, a Spanish guy with a wife who, he says, lives mostly in Spain, won't give me a key to my door but I'll worry about that later.)

At least the leak gets me out of bed.

Having caught the coach from Oxford to London and stayed with my sister a few days in outer suburban dreariness, I'd found this room in West Kensington in the *Evening Standard* small ads – £1 10s a week and a short walk from my favourite underground line – the District and Circle, where all the most glamorous addresses were, I had decided. Okay, my nearest station was the distinctly unfashionable Baron's Court next to the unglamorous Hammersmith flyover, but for 30s I could hardly expect Sloane Square.

There's enough money in my post office savings book to last for a month by which time I must have a job or else I go back to my mum, the cat, the budgie and our home – a 16ft caravan on a small estate in Botley, an Oxford backwater.

I have to make this work. Mum can't afford to support me any more and who wants to live in a bloody caravan anyway? Not me.

At 11 a.m. I have my first interview. Well, to be honest, the only interview I've got lined up. For the only job I want to do. Ever. But I don't stand a chance. But I've got to try. Otherwise, I'll never know.

So I dry my hair and curse the kinks that appear, and put on the warpaint: Rimmel Truly Fair make-up for combination skin; Boots Cream Blusher, Truly Fair powder compact (anti-shine); bright pink lipstick (pinched from Mother's small and ancient make up collection), Boots Powder Eyeshadow in Shimmer Blue. All fine. Shaking hands, stab eye at last hurdle – Rimmel Stay Put Mascara in Brownish-Black. Bugger. Not that stay put then – as my eye streams the mascara ruins everything. Have to start again. Bugger! I'm going to be late.

10.15 a.m. Run down Gliddon Road, across the Talgarth Road and join the crowds jostling into the tube on their way to work. Feel the rush! I'm actually part of the London rush hour. How fantastic is that? When you've come from living in a caravan and then you leave your mansion block and walk down the streets of West London to catch the tube to get to work, and you can actually mingle with Londoners at last, and pretend to be one – well, that's amazing. Even more amazing to get out at Blackfriars and walk down towards Ludgate Circus and FLEET STREET. Fleet Street!

I'm 11 and it's my first visit to London, and I'm standing on Fleet Street with my mother and her friend Mrs Hill.

As I don't talk a lot, ever, they aren't to know that
I'm almost passing out with excitement to be here at
last. With the help of one of my life's many decent
coincidences, it turns out that Mrs Hill's oldest son
works in an office right on the street itself. So here we
are, waiting for him to take us to lunch.

There was a year, around the age of 8, when I wanted
to be a stable girl, but two years ago I decided I want to
be a journalist and that's been my career decided ever
since. Nothing more, nothing less will do. So just to
stand here, near the *Daily Express* and the *Daily Mail*
and *Reuters* ...

'Do you think he's a reporter? Is he Cassandra?
Do you think she's a journalist? Where's the Cheshire
Cheese? Where's the Wig and Pen?' all this said to
myself, not out loud, I don't like to be a nuisance.

This is the only place to be, I have to be here. I can't
wait to grow up.

Strange, now, to think that a walk down grubby old Fleet
Street was enough to begin the process of turning me from
a shy no-hoper child into, several years later, a walking
advertisement for Feel the Fear and Do It Anyway.

Thank God for aspiration and ambition, the fantastic surge
of anticipation that comes in around adolescence. The blind
faith that says 'I am special!' and the ignorance that allows
you to say 'I can do anything I want!'

Without that, a large helping of luck, and the undoubted
advantage that my ambition was to work on a teen pop

magazine rather than be the next Simon Jenkins of *The Times* or Katherine Whitehorn of *The Observer*, I would probably still be in Botley today.

By the time I cross Ludgate Circus and begin the journey down Farringdon Street, I'm not so much walking as wobbling along, as my knees have given way with nerves. I would ask the way now but I can't because my voice has disappeared along with my bravado. I'm holding my *A-to-Z* but I'm too embarrassed to look at it as I don't want people to think I'm new around here. My stabbed eye aches a bit. Also, I am itching.

It's the suit. A quite ghastly two-piece skirt suit, knee-length, turquoise (yes, turquoise) in the style of Chanel but actually from Oxford Market, price £1 5s. Nearly a whole week's cleaning wages for my mother. Made of some tweed-like material, thick, unyielding, ITCHY.

Also of course, I'm sweating. Boiling hot London day, bulky jacket, tights, blouse complete with pussycat neck bow tied too tightly, long sleeves, cheap nylon. So I'm sweating with the suit and sweating with nerves and wondering if I've got BO and dark patches showing through my jacket yet, and in this state I arrive at New Fleetway House – a less than prepossessing concrete office block nearly underneath the Holborn Viaduct. Shall I just leave now? I don't want this job anyway. Who'd want to work in a place like this? Well, I do. Actually I do, very much.

Having negotiated the utilitarian entrance, the manual lift and a short stretch of windowless corridor, it really is like a *Wizard of Oz* or *Through the Looking Glass* moment, when all suddenly becomes light and beauty and bustle and glamour, the dream turns good, if rather quirky.

I stand like Dorothy/Alice surrounded by the Beautiful People who make *Fabulous Magazine* come true every week. I know them all because *Fabulous Magazine* is so cool it actually prints photos of the people who work there on its pages; it makes them its own mini-celebs. And, as I said, I am a reader. A fully paid up, order it from my newsagent, reader, from the very first issue which had The Beatles on the cover.

And I can see John Fearn, the art editor with the bowtie; Maureen 'Mo' who does the letters page. Heather Kirby the fashion editor. My God, there's June Southworth who writes the *Fab* features and gets to mix with the stars each week. And here's this ethereal gorgeous person, Anne Wilson, who is the 'Ed's Sec' (for this is how 'editor's secretary' is written each week in the mag). Anne Wilson is famous to us readers because she is so slim and lovely she is often used as a model on the pages of *Fabulous*. And now Anne Wilson is drifting over to me, smiling at me. It's her job I have come to try to win.

What a joke. What a nerve.

'Can I help you?'

Grab the side of a desk to stop myself running away.

'JudithWillscomeforjobinterview.' All in a rush.

Just smile, Mother had said. I smile but my lips have stuck to my gums and I can't undo them. My suit's the worst thing. They're all wearing flower power, floaty things – even the men. God, what can possibly be worse than wearing the Wrong Clothes?

Then after a while Anne leads me through the inner sanctum door and there she is. The most envied woman in the teenage world. Unity. Unity Hall. The editor. Or 'Ed' as she is known to us readers. Her Ed's Letter each week tells tales of who she's met, which pop hero has come to the office, what great press parties she's been to. Her life is so glamorous it's even off the scale of my vivid imagination and here she sits before me in her *Fabulous* office at her *Fabulous* desk looking *Fabulous* – if with a slightly dodgy Cleopatra haircut and eyebrows, I later bitchily decide.

God knows what she thinks of my suit, my sweat, my accent, my red eye, my sheer all-embracing inability to talk or persuade her as to why she should employ me; my lack of personality or a trace of common sense.

'Previous experience as a secretary, dear?'

None.

'Qualifications?'

Poor A levels in English Literature, which may or may not be useful here, and Economic History, which definitely won't, and shorthand and typing.

It was the shorthand and typing which was almost to be my downfall. For after a fifteen-minute interview, Unity decided that I had to have a practical test.

'Just get your notepad out, dear, and I'll dictate you a little letter and you can use Anne's typewriter to type it out.'

My brain froze and hands shook as she dictated a letter to Cyril Maitland, *Fabulous*'s photographer in Los Angeles. I was so excited to have a letter to Cyril Maitland dictated to me by the editor of *Fab* that actually taking the dictation was not possible. When I came to type it up, all there was on the pad were a few meaningless squiggles in no known shorthand language. So I sat at Anne's Olympia and decided to improvise the missing bits. In other words, I made it all up.

After I'd finished my fiction, an hour passed, during which time I sat, virtually in an hypnotic trance brought on by my nerves, a dreadful thirst and utter disbelief that I'd managed to get into this space, the holy grail of my young teen years. At some point someone offered me a cup of tea but I had to refuse – what if I spilled it down my front?

Then I'm summoned back into Unity's office for the verdict.

She's talking to me about how bad my shorthand test was. And I'm agreeing, and nodding and trying to look okay about it, and babbling, 'Well, never mind, it was great to meet you; thanks for seeing me anyway …'.

She finally gets a word in, shouting.

'NO DEAR – I DO want you to work for me! I'M OFFERING YOU THE POST.'

'WHAT DID YOU SAY?'

'I want you to have the job!'

'But why? – you just said you haven't seen a worse effort at transcribing in years!'

'YES, DEAR – well I expect you'll improve, and I like you,' Unity boomed. 'In fact I think your letter to Cyril was better than mine!'

I reckoned she just felt sorry for me and hadn't the heart to turn me away. It wasn't until years later that I cottoned on to the fact that all the best magazine stories are made up, so she no doubt thought my letter showed true promise.

And thus I was to start as Ed's Sec in one week's time.
I'd landed the job of my dreams.

WOW, COOL, GROOVY, WOW, COOL, FAB!
* I'm the new Ed's Sec of *Fabulous*.
* I work just off Fleet Street.
* I don't have to get in until 10 a.m.
* I am earning £4 10s a week on a three-month trial
  basis.
* Soon I may be able to afford a new dress, a floaty dress.
* I can talk to John, Anne (who is still at *Fab*, promoted,
  appropriately, to beauty editor) and Mo, just by
  shouting from my desk. Not that I would. As John says
  a few days into my new job, 'What did Unity employ
  you for? – You wouldn't say boo to a goose.'
* I can even see Doug Perry when he comes in once
  a week. He works for Radio Luxembourg (London),
  which is an even more glam job than working for *Fab*,
  and writes the *Fab* Luxy column. He's rather nice.
* And I might get to see some of the stars who come in to
  see us hoping for a paragraph or two, or even a whole
  feature written about them.
* I now know the true meaning of the phrase 'deliriously
  happy'. For I truly am.
* Well, 75 per cent deliriously happy; 25 per cent shit
  scared. How the hell am I going to pull it off?

two

Now and Always

AUTUMN 1967

Brian Epstein died in August. BBC Radio 1 was launched on 30 September. It was a Saturday, but I got up early to listen as Tony Blackburn introduced the first song – The Move, 'Flowers in the Rain'. The leak above my bed was mended, the drip stopped, but the landlord still hasn't given me a key to my bedroom door.

Now let's talk about Doug Perry.

We only had one date.

He asked me out, but instead of doing the sensible thing and just allowing myself to be taken on a date, what did I do?

Yes, of course – I invited him round for a meal at the bedsit. Of course I did.

It did make sense to me in that split second I found myself inviting him so it's completely useless now to want to scream at my young self, 'WHAT ON EARTH ARE YOU THINKING OF? DON'T DO IT.'

I'd been in London for three months and was yet to make any female friends in town. Perry was the first person of either sex who had shown any interest in me whatsoever. And I just wanted to be grown up and to be liked and to be cool, and I thought that was what nice grown up cool people did – invite friends round to their pad for a meal.

But there was a problem, the first in quite a long line of problems relating to my liaison with Mr Perry – I couldn't cook: hell, I could not cook. Years of moving home and family ructions and a mother who spent long spells in various hospitals with depression and other ills had ensured that somehow being taught the rudiments just never happened.

Mother also spent a fair bit of her civilian life with her friend Mrs Hill, whom she'd met in the Ashurst Clinic in Oxford. Mrs Hill had undergone a frontal lobotomy to try to curb her antisocial urges, which included trying to kill cats and other small mammals. For many years, from when I was about 9 to about 17, Mother had a strange fascination for this woman.

'I Put a Spell on You'. Was that Nina Simone?

By the time I was 11, old enough to show an interest in how food got on the table, we were actually living with Mrs Hill and her three youngest children. And to live successfully as an outsider in the Hill household, you had to a) obey the rules and b) be neither seen nor heard. So activities such as playing music, making a noise or creating mess or disruption to the household of any kind – including cooking – were out.

Later, we left the Hill home in Botley and for two years Mum and Dad tried to make another go of living together. They split up again, Mum and I moved to the caravan, and I still didn't cook, except for one time when I was nearly 16.

Mum's tired. She does all these cleaning jobs and then she walks up the steep road to the top of Botley where Mrs Hill lives, then back down again. I think I'll cook our tea today. It can't be that hard. She's bought two small breaded fish fillets and chips.

So I turn on the small gas ring and the grill. I grill the chips and one minute they're white and pasty, the next minute they're black. I fry the fillets but I don't know you have to put fat in the frying pan and they stick to the bottom. She's sitting there, watching *Nationwide*, and waiting. So I serve it up. The chips are still not cooked inside. The fish is in small pieces. She smiles, trying hard not to mind about the waste of money, and we have a tin of pilchards instead. And I'm definitely not going to be cooking for her any more, well, not for a long while.

I could not cook, and I didn't cook. But that didn't stop me inviting Doug Perry round for dinner. I offered him steak, chips, vegetables, apple pie and custard. I remember telling him the menu when I invited him, standing there in the *Fab* offices like some demented waiter. I thought men liked steak and I liked apple pie, and it all sounded straightforward enough. Poor sod, he probably thought he'd fill his belly with decent food then have his wicked way with me.

Poor man. What kind of a message was it giving out to him – making him come round to my bedsit on our first date, plying him with plonk, inviting him to sit on the bed (to be fair to myself, there was nowhere else to sit except on the picnic chairs that were set up with the picnic table for our meal in the small empty square between the bed and the TV – good job we were both thin as rakes). I didn't want to sleep with him, hadn't even thought of it, but of course he wasn't to know that.

I didn't think to try the apartment cooker beforehand, nor did I have enough gumption to borrow a cookbook from somewhere and bone up about cooking steak and the rest of it. In those days you couldn't just call in a takeaway, there was no such thing. And, anyway, I didn't have a phone.

But I did shop for the food and a nice bottle of Mateus Rose, buy the picnic table, lay it with my best Habitat cutlery (happily by this time my wages had gone up to £6 a week having, miraculously, passed my three-month trial). I didn't realise that Habitat was quite trendy – it just happened to be the nearest shop I could find that sold household items.

All I had to do was cook the food. I would actually even now prefer not to recall too much detail of the preparation and mastication of that meal because it still makes me blush today, but it was, basically, Hell's Kitchen combined with Junior Masterchef, worst of, multiplied by a million. As the awfulness of the food sank into both our stomachs and brains, conversation seemed increasingly superfluous and pointless, and so in profound silence Doug did his best to eat the inedible, then he left. Didn't even try it on. So at least the meal served a purpose of sorts.

Henceforth when he came in to *Fab* to do his weekly column we would avoid each other to such a degree that I don't think I ever saw him again. Turned out he had a steady girlfriend all along anyway. Maybe was even engaged, I recall. So he got his just desserts with that meal in every sense of the word. And it probably helped me to begin understanding that there are certain things you can't wing without a little bit of knowledge and/or expertise. I should have been taken out for a nice drink and a Wimpy, or a ham omelette at The Golden Egg and then things could have turned out differently. But then I'd never have been free to date Jason Eddie.

EARLY 1968

The wife only appeared once in six months, my room door key never materialised, and finally the Spaniard tried to rape me.

I wouldn't let him. Perhaps he was so surprised at just how determined I was that I wouldn't be raped, that it stopped him in his tracks a bit, but it was lucky that the apartment doorbell rang mid fight, the Spaniard vanished into his own sitting room, I ran to the door and it was Jason Eddie, come to take me out for a drink.

I never told him what he'd interrupted, or why I wanted to get an *Evening Standard* and find somewhere else to live, RIGHT NOW. He must have wondered why I looked dishevelled and flushed and he did ask what had happened but I couldn't tell him because, I think, I couldn't face him and the Spaniard having a fight. I once witnessed my father and my brother fighting, blood pouring down my dad's face, and I didn't want a repeat. I never told a soul for years what happened in that bedsit, in fact like with so many of the less groovy things that happened to me in the next few years, I put it right out of my brain. NO need for counselling (not in those days); just get on with life, forget it. You move to London, things like that sometimes happen. They help you change from naïve country bumpkin to wordly wise woman, is the best way I could look at it.

It's only now that I look back and wonder if the way I behaved (example: the Doug Perry scenario) gave people the wrong impression.

I remember chatting with the Spaniard, being friendly with him, testing my powers of socialising which up until my move to London had been non-existent. I was also beginning to realise that I could, if I tried hard, look quite reasonably attractive, so perhaps I was unconsciously testing my erratic powers of flirtation with the guy who was, I have to say, not fanciable in the slightest – short, fat, garlicky, not my type. On the other hand, how I behaved to him might have had no influence on the outcome at all – he probably would just have pounced on any female around at the time, whatever she did or didn't do or say.

I never saw him again. The next morning he had disappeared – a curt one-line note was left on the kitchen table to say he had gone to Spain for a holiday and within less than two weeks I was moved out, with the help of Eddie and his old pink-and-yellow convertible and ensconced in Avonmore Road, West Kensington, in a good-sized double bedsit (this time complete with its own tiny kitchen) with a nice Polish landlady, Mrs Filipinski.

One tube stop nearer town, one more lesson learnt – seemed symbolic, progression of a sort.

I had met Jason Eddie at my first *Fab* party. These parties were legendary at Fleetway House – Unity would invite all the staff, a small selection of readers, her mates from Fleet Street proper (her husband, Owen Summers was a Fleet Street big boy crime writer and they were one of the first glam media couples), and as many pop stars and budding pop stars as she could round up.

Jason had come along with his brother. After a few minutes he swaggered towards me.

'Hi! I'm Jason Eddie.' Held out his hand. 'Who are you?'

'I'm Judy, Unity's secretary. I know who you are.'

From that moment he didn't let me out of his sight, and after a while had me almost believing that I was the most fascinating person in the room – obviously not true. I was flattered. And I had a special interest in this man.

He was nothing special to look at. Medium, stocky build, dark blonde hair, nice smile like his brother, fancied himself as a singer, like his brother. What attracted me to him was his GSOH – and the fact that his brother was the person I had dreamed of day and night from the age of nearly 13, whose face had adorned my bedroom walls since I first saw a photo of him on the front cover of a magazine, whose records I'd nearly worn out playing them on my Dansette, and who still had the power to turn me into a dumbstruck fan every time I met him. Jason's brother was the legendary 'UK Elvis' – Billy Fury.

> I'm in the newsagents at the bottom of Botley Hill. I've just got off the school bus and I have a shilling and I'm going to buy some sweets. I wait to be served and in front of me is the loveliest face I've ever seen. On a magazine called *Marilyn*. This is it – love at first sight. I don't know who it is. But I have to buy the magazine and find out.
>
> Billy Fury. He's a singer. He has a record out. I'm going to save up and buy it, and then a record player. If there is someone this gorgeous in the world, then life might be worth living after all.

What Fury's voice or music was like wasn't really going to matter – but as it turned out, I liked that too. And Mum bought me my first LP – *Billy Fury* – for my 14th birthday.

Jason had left Liverpool a week or two before we met, and arrived in the Smoke to seek his own celebrity in the recording industry. By using his brother, he got an invite to the *Fab* party and began what I now realise was serious networking. Although I was still only Ed's Sec, and pretty useless to him really, he wasn't to know that so he went after me quite determinedly. Perhaps he did fancy me a bit but certainly at the start this would have been a secondary consideration. So there was this wonderful serendipity – we were both madly using each other while pretending not to.

It all worked out rather well for a time – he got to record a single, 'Heart and Soul', which was actually played on the radio and wasn't too bad at all. He did some gigs, became a kind of 1960s Z-list celebrity, and I had plenty of fun off the back of his success.

Riding round town in his Zodiac (or whatever similar car of the day it was; I only ever noted the colour) beat the bus any day, and I also had the kudos of taking Billy Fury's brother home to visit Mum, who by this time was living with my grandmother back in Buckingham, and who had always been almost as big a fan of Billy Fury as I was.

Because of Jason, I also got to know Billy and his personal manager, Hal Carter, Hal's wife Sam and his team of helpers and other artistes.

Hal and Sam lived in a small flat in Osbaldestone Road, Stoke Newington. By the time their first baby, Warren, was born, we were quite good friends and I began babysitting for them from time to time; an arrangement which came to an abrupt and understandable end one winter evening a while later. Warren was asleep in the bedroom, being kept warm with a gas stove, and I was in the living room engrossed in TV as usual.

When Hal and Sam returned I could hear her screaming before they even started up the stairs. I hadn't noticed that the gas stove had somehow gone wrong, the bedroom was filled with smoke and any moment would have been alight. I was still sitting there in front of the TV surrounded by the escaping, choking fumes, and I hadn't even noticed.

Little Warren was ok, as it turned out, but I was quickly bundled from the apartment and Hal and Sam found themselves a new babysitter.

They were still, charitable people, happy to be friends with me, and I was even invited to baby Warren's christening in July 1969 – along with my new friend Gordon Coxhill from the *New Musical Express*, and Billy and his new wife, a woman called, irritatingly, Judith. One of only two photos I have of myself with Fury was taken at this event, outside the church at the top of the Carter's street. There I stand, just behind Fury and Judith, wearing my Biba velvet floppy hat and a rather stupid faraway expression. The other photo of me with Fury was taken when I was 16 years old, four years earlier.

I've just had the best news anyone could give me. Billy Fury is appearing this Christmas in pantomime! He's going to be Aladdin. BUT guess where? Can you believe – he is going to come here, to our New Theatre at Oxford!! This is just amazing. I can't really believe it's true.

Precisely 1.5 miles from where I live, in our caravan at Botley Road Estate, Billy Fury himself is going to come every day for weeks and weeks and weeks, and be Aladdin. Right through until February 1966. Of all the places his manager could have chosen, he chose here. Thank you, God! Thank you Larry Parnes! Thank you world and life.

You've made me a very, very, happy person.

So I stand, shaking with nerves, at the stage door sometime early in December as he is due to arrive for rehearsals. This I have discovered because his backing group, The Gamblers, who are also in the show, have rented a houseboat on the Isis for the duration of the gig, from Salter Brothers – whose manager happens to be my brother, Rob! The Gamblers have told him all the dates I need to know …

And the Vanden Plas car arrives and there he is – medium tall, very slim, wearing a trilby with a feather in it – Billy Fury. And there is just one fan waiting … me.

Oh – and my mother, armed with camera. I just manage to speak,

'Please Billy will you pose for a photo!'

'Yes of course,' a low, quiet voice with an almost American accent. So the deed is done, then Billy disappears inside the stage door.

My mother gets the film developed and I am sure the photo of Billy and I will be blurred, or not come out – but it does, and it's perfect. Except for the stupid expression on my face.

A long time afterwards my mother says he had birdshit on his hat, but I didn't notice that.

Once or twice Jason and I visited Billy and Judith at her home in North London – usually because Jason, whose real name was Albert, was short of money or wanted Billy to help him further his career.

The first time, we were ushered into the sitting room and after a few minutes Billy appeared, as shy and quiet as ever. Every time we went, I would sit there spellbound to be in the same room, as an acquaintance, with Billy, his girl and his brother.

But after a few months of being, there is no other word for it, pestered, Billy, quite understandably, began to get slightly peeved with his brother. I remember once Jason receiving a letter in the post from Billy, which he showed me, incensed.

I read the note, which gently pointed out that Billy had helped Albert several times and hadn't a great deal of spare cash at the moment. He suggested Albert return to Liverpool, get a job, save up some more money and return to London another time. And he signed it, love Ron (his real name). I actually found myself near tears when I read that letter, in Billy's scrawl, as I agreed with every word he said but I couldn't say so as Albert was there ranting over it and calling his brother every swear word in the book.

'What's the matter with him – he's got plenty of money, what's the matter.'

In fact, Fury didn't have a lot of money – his career had nosedived since The Beatles had revolutionised the pop world and he was struggling to earn money by gigging in smallish places, while battling severe ill health and a weak heart. He used to come off stage near collapse.

Not long after, Albert did what Billy had suggested – went back home, and later I found out from Hal that Albert had never officially left his wife, he'd simply been given 'leave' to try his luck in London for a while. I was quite shocked as I'd never intended to be 'the other woman' and yet so far since moving to London the only male contact I'd had had been with an engaged man, a married man and, of course, a would-be rapist.

Luckily, I didn't care about Jason enough to be that sad at his departure. It took me about two weeks to realise I was quite glad he'd gone, on several levels.

I realised that he was not appreciative of his brother in the slightest at the time. I believe he was jealous of the Fury success and incredulous that it hadn't happened for him. I was also mildly annoyed that he'd lied to me (or at best, avoided telling me the truth) about his situation back home.

Did Jason Eddie have talent? Well, he had nowhere near the looks or charisma of his brother. He could sing a bit – but put him in X Factor today and he would probably be lucky to make the live shows.

Because of my acquaintance with Hal and through my own career, which was ever so slightly on the move itself, I met Fury several more times after Jason left.

Yet I never could get over the fan/star thing – once a fan, always a fan – and I don't recall ever having one sensible conversation with him. I never did interview him for *Fab* or any other publication because it would have been a disaster. But he was a lovely, lovely man – gentle, nature-loving and very un-starry. He even ended up, before his very early death at 42, living just a few miles from me, down in the Welsh Borders. He had a farm and used to spend his time birdwatching (yes, mother, it probably really was bird poo on his hat) and rounding up sheep. We should have got on really well – pity I just couldn't make that leap from fan to true friend.

three

The Good, the Bad – and the Bizarre

1968

1968 is racing along. The Shadows have split up. London Bridge has been sold to America. Cliff's got religion – he's been delivering sermons with Billy Graham. Bobby Kennedy and Tony Hancock are dead. Hell! Mickey from The Monkees has married Samantha Juste of Top of the Pops, and the fans are crying into their colas. And I'm in need of a friend.

These were Monkee days – Mike Nesmith, Peter Tork, Davy Jones, the English one who had once been in *Coronation Street* as a kid, and Mickey Dolenz – were the first huge boy band from America, the first 'manufactured' pop band ever, brought together, via an advert, for a fun-and-music TV series. Perfect for 13 year olds. Because of them, the magazine offices were besieged with teens and the phone rang off the hook.

I spent many an hour reading the mail begging us to get autographs, arrange meetings and so on. I realised how much better I felt, working in the business rather than being a hopeless fan. However, while they made nice, bop-able pop music singles like 'I'm a Believer', I couldn't get that excited over The Monkees myself.

Apparently I met Davy Jones, who must have made such a great impression on me that I can't remember a thing about where we met, or indeed anything about him at all except he was very short and quite harmless. Certainly not hearththrob material in my book. And I only know for sure that I met him because I announced, importantly, in my fan club biography under the heading 'claims to fame': 'I have dined with Davy Jones'.

Yes, by this time, Judy Wills didn't have a real friend, but she had her own official fan club. Because of the huge interest in The Monkees, and because I was sometimes photographed modelling clothes in the pages of *Fab*, I started to get a lot of letters addressed not to the editor, but to me. Letters that would spell out how wonderful I was, how pretty, how nice, and so on. Being naïve, and with huge potential to be big-headed, I truly believed that the readers thought I was great.

So it was that a couple of girls called Tina and Vivienne from South London started up a fan club for me – I still have a copy of the biography of myself that I sent them listing my fave colours, film stars, food etc. I have no memory at all of ever liking Volvo cars, Julie Christie, or Gilbert and Sullivan – but apparently, I liked them all enough to record the fact in my biography along with my dinner date with the Jones boy.

Not long after the setting up of my fan club, Tina and Vivienne wrote to me again, asking if I knew anyone who would like to be a member. They were obviously having recruitment difficulties and, I believe, the enterprise folded not all that many weeks later.

Now of course, rereading the few letters I've saved down the years, I can see that all the readers wanted was to butter me up and get me to get them an autograph or, optimistically, a meeting, with their fave Monkee, or a pair of their dirty underpants.

Still, not many nonentities can boast having once had their own official fan club so I feel quite proud.

Another reader with whom I became friendly was a woman of about 35 called Leni Coster who ran the Richard Chamberlain UK fan club from her home in Cowes, Isle of Wight. Chamberlain had long been one of my heroes – in fact he was the very first person on TV on whom I had a crush as soon as I saw him in the long-running US series *Dr Kildare*; the first male I ever fancied before Billy Fury came along.

I've always been a sucker for a good bedside manner and he seemed to have that in spades and was unthreateningly clean cut and good looking with dyed blonde hair, perfect teeth and a square jaw – just the job, all of that, when you're 11 and 12.

I'd look forward to *Dr Kildare* every week on BBC, counting down the days and hours until it came on at 8 p.m. on Wednesdays. But every week it was a tussle between Richard Hill and me to see who would be triumphant in the sitting room – would I win and be allowed to watch it, or would he win and send me crying to the bedroom?

Mrs Hill had three children still at home – Clive, who was around 20, Veronica, who was about 16, and Richard, who was about 15.

I wish we didn't have to live here. It's not our house and all I get is nasty whispered words from all three of her children when they think no-one else can hear. 'Why don't you go back where you came from?' 'This is OUR house – what are you doing here?'

Richard hates me the most. He finds ways to upset me. Any way he can. And when it works he grins his horrid grin and I hate him too. Why did I ever let him know I like *Dr Kildare*? He always wants something on the other channel now.

Last week he put salt in my tea, and salted my supper so much I couldn't eat it. He sneaks into the room I share with Veronica and hides my stuff or tears the pages of my magazines. The worst thing is, he kicks

Christopher Columbus because he knows I love that cat more than even I love *Dr Kildare*.

By the time I was 13 in August 1962, I was beginning to change from complete tomboy to someone with the first traces of femininity. My mum bought me my first pack of two bras.

My dad, who lived in Banbury and was allowed to have me to stay for a weekend once a month, had bought me a couple of dresses and paid for my first visit to a hairdresser, where I had been given a (truly horrendous) cut and perm, and had also allowed me a tube of pink lipstick and a mascara wand, these last three much to my mum's disgust. Not that I ever went out anywhere.

Around this time Richard's manner towards me unexpectedly changed and I'd notice him watching me, watching me.

He's tall now, he's very tall. Lately he's tried to be nice to me and I don't know why. Where's Mum? Where's Mrs Hill even? Why am I here in this house with just Richard bloody Hill?

I've come in the sitting room to find the *Radio Times* and he's followed me and he's shut the door. And I want to avoid looking at him but as I aim for the door he grabs my arm.

'You look nice today!' he says in his best sarcastic tone.

And he grabs my newly formed left breast encased in its new bra and he squeezes and squeezes until it hurts so much, tears of pain and anger come.

I'm like a rabbit, caught in the headlights of his
gloating, taunting, blue steel eyes. I can't move, I'm
frozen, I can't stop him, I can't speak. But I can feel,
inside, I can feel hate.

Of course I never said a word because I didn't want to put
my mother in the position of deciding whether to tell and
get chucked out.

My obsession with Kildare faded a little over the next
couple of years as Billy Fury became my No. 1 hero, but
only ended when the TV series did in 1966 and Richard
Chamberlain disappeared from my small screen forever – or
at least until *The Thorn Birds* came along many years later.

Six or seven years on, Leni and I struck up a correspondence
– again we both had something to offer the other – I organised
for details of her fan club to appear in *Fab*, while she took me
on a fan club jaunt to meet Richard Chamberlain. Somehow
or other she had wangled an invitation to take a few members
along to Richard's debut as a serious Shakespearean actor,
playing Hamlet in Birmingham rep. I found the production –
and I have to say Chamberlain's acting – boring as hell and
nearly went to sleep but rallied when the call came along the
stalls that Richard would meet a few of us backstage after
the performance.

So off I went, bleary-eyed, but still oddly excited to meet
my one-time hero. He was standing in the centre of a large
communal dressing room, still in his full make-up, talking to
a young male companion. As he turned round to greet us,
I saw straight into his eyes, which seemed to say, 'I'll put

up with this but that's about it,' and it came to me in that one thunderstruck moment that my teenage crush had been completely wasted on this man. Not just because he was bored and distant (actors who meet and greet fans should always be good enough actors to at least *appear* to be pleased to be meeting them) but because he was, quite obviously, gay or, as I would have put it in those days, homosexual.

Why had I never realised it before? Why did it matter? I just felt I had spent the first two years of my pubescence lusting after someone who could never have returned the feelings even if I had been ten years older, ten stars more gorgeous and ten times more intelligent. Let's be honest, I hadn't been his 'fan' because of his acting talent, or his integrity, or his intelligence. I had been a fan because of the sex thing or, at least, the 'love' or 'infatuation' thing.

I felt disappointed without yet even having spoken to him. I felt sorry for all the millions of fans like me who had wasted hours fancying a guy who could never fancy them back.

We exchanged a few stilted pleasantries, shook hands, then I left the room and got the coach or whatever back to London; I don't think Leni ever realised how my early teenage dreams had been crushed that night.

In later years I spent several fun evenings with my gay workmate Richard at his club in Victoria, where gay couples of both sexes would dance the night away and I would be upset only because I hadn't got anyone to dance with. But I didn't feel any more awkward than I had done when, on several occasions as a young teen in Oxfordshire, I had similarly been a wallflower at hetero dances.

So why was I so disappointed about Chamberlain? I suppose a bit like in the days when George Michael pretended not to be gay because he (or his team) was worried it would affect his fanbase, Richard Chamberlain or his press office had, apparently, concealed his sexual preferences with fabricated stories of which woman he was 'dating' planted in the press, and so on, and I felt cheated. I'd rather have known the truth so I could choose whether to stay loyal to him or to give my virgin adoration to someone who might, eventually, have wanted it. Well, stranger things have happened – Gary Numan married a fan, after all.

Work acquaintances aside, I really still didn't have any proper friends or a boyfriend after Jason disappeared, and was, though I didn't want to admit it to myself, quite lonely.

As I was still babysitting for Hal Carter from time to time, I would bump into Jimmy Campbell, another of Hal's small stable of music acts. Jimmy, like Billy, came from Liverpool and having been with a band called the Kirkbys was trying to make it on his own. He was a fantastic songwriter, played guitar and had a plaintive little voice. He was the Ed Sheeran of his day, except he never really took off at the time.

Now he is regarded by many as a 'lost' talent and has a cult following of his own – just Google him. Anyway, he looked lovely and I went to his home a couple of times when he had parties or friends round, and did what I could to attract his attention (which probably consisted of wearing too much make-up, too few clothes and overlong false eyelashes), but he was completely disinterested in me, though at the time

I refused to believe it. I kidded myself he was just very shy (which he probably was too).

After one fruitless all-night get together at his house during which I'd managed to keep myself awake on the off-chance that this would be the night he would realise how fab I was, I sat, dizzy with lack of sleep and disappointment, on a train to my sister's in Perivale, crying my eyes out – having finally realised it was never going to happen and that I had made a fool of myself. I don't think I ever saw him again. I daresay he used Hal radar to disappear whenever I might be going up to Stoke Newington.

I wanted to be liked/loved and found attractive, but the men I liked and found attractive didn't want to know. I just didn't seem to be able to behave around men in any kind of normal way. I wasn't capable of analysing the problem at the time, but now I can. I was just too needy and lacking in even minimal confidence, which made me act in various types of non-me way. I would be, either in turn or all at once, distant, superior, fawning all over them, coming on strong, trembling with nerves, talking too loud, telling inappropriate jokes, but never, ever, would I just act like a rational human being. I was the original Miranda Hart, but disguised with long hair and miniskirts. I must have freaked them out.

Despite this, I had my standards about the quality of young man I would be prepared to date, which only made matters worse. My married sister Ann set me up on a couple of evenings with people she knew, but unless they were 'in the business' (show business or media) I found them all deadly dull. With a dull man I was fine, I could behave normally, but I could never be bothered to see him a second time. One in particular was called Mick, a well-meaning, tubby guy from Yorkshire, a member of the Ramblers Association. I remember thinking that if ever I listed rambling as a top hobby I would cut my own throat.

Jason Eddie had been the exception to these random dating rules and behaviours of mine – but I can see now, it was because although I had enough reasons to want to be with him for the while we were together, I just wasn't crazy enough about him to act crazy. So by default he more or less got the actual me.

I no doubt could have done with mindfulness therapy, or chamomile tea, or hot yoga, or reiki, but none of that was easily available/heard of in the late '60s. So I just had to wait and calm down slowly over time in a vaguely organic, one-step-forward two-steps-back kind of fashion.

So, understandably alone in the evenings for weeks at a time, I would go back to the bedsit to watch *Top of the Pops* and Jimmy Savile on my black-and-white telly with its fuzzy picture, or catch up on writing, or listen to BBC Radio 1 or Radio Luxembourg on my transistor radio. Being on my own in 'my own place' was almost a luxury and I was never bored, but often I would wonder when the 'happening' times were really going to happen.

That said, I looked forward to going to the office every single day, and I also realised that if I worked hard at improving my look, this might cancel out the negative effect of my personality bypass. So I grew my hair, spent hours doing and redoing my make-up and read all the features I could find on 'how to improve your confidence'.

While this didn't, certainly at first, help me get a guy, it had an unexpected bonus. Fashion editor Heather began asking me to model clothes in the magazine. I flattered myself and dared to hope that it was because of my supreme gorgeousness, but in reality it was mainly because I was dead skinny, my services came free, and agency models were quite expensive.

Even so, it was great to get out of the office and be photographed by some of the up-and-coming fashion photographers of the day. No, I never got near Bailey or Donovan (Terence, not the folk singer) but it was still fun – and we did get John Swannell, who later became one of the top celeb and fashion photographers around. I still have the first spread of photos of me in *Fab* titled 'Groovy Girl', and on the back of 'my' page was a photo of The Beatles! Gave me quite a buzz.

Sometimes wannabe or nearly-there pop stars would come along and model clothes with me. One of these was a tiny blonde girl with pleasant but not devastating looks, bubbly but not at all sure of herself, who was trying to make it as a singer. I didn't catch her name on the day but when the photos were published complete with captions, it turned out to be Elaine Paige. Once I did a modelling session with Steve Ellis, lead singer of the band Love Affair, who had a massive hit with 'Everlasting Love'. You can see on the photos that my eyes were swollen and red – that was because I'd just found out Billy Fury had got engaged to his girl Judith. I knew I never stood a chance myself, but it still upset me.

I enjoyed modelling so much that I toyed with the idea of leaving *Fab* and becoming a model. My biggest coup was appearing on the cover of the young woman's glossy magazine, *Honey* – seeing myself on the newspaper stands down Fleet Street was a boost to my ego, for sure, and occasional moonlighting modelling stints for the national press followed. For example, I became one of the *Daily Mirror*'s Gorgeous Girls. Every day, a 'gorgeous girl' – in theory spotted walking around town, but in truth offered a fiver to pose – would appear in the paper, on, I think, page 7. I guess it was the pre-cursor of all the tabloid page threes, except we were all fully clothed. They got my name wrong, which prompted my dad to write to them from his headquarters – a council flat in Oxford – to complain, about which I was very embarrassed. Wills, Wallace? Who cared? Well, I cared a bit, but I wasn't going to admit it. At least it gave Sally Cork, the new *Fab* beauty editor, a smile.

She, too, had been photographed for the same feature, but it was my photo they used rather than hers. I never spoke to her about it but she would have been justified in being a bit miffed, especially as she was prettier than me.

Kent Gavin, the photographer on that assignment, took a marginal shine to me, perhaps mistaking my habitual silence in his presence for a Greta Garbo kind of allure, rather than my habitual 'being terrified' mode. I thought he was quite good looking and suave in a tabloid-photographer dirty cuffs kind of way. I also liked the attention he gave me as he was one of the first well-known Fleet Street photographers, knew everyone who mattered in the media, was an 'older man' (probably in his mid-30s which is ancient when you're 18 or so), and I felt a bit of his aura of fame and supreme confidence warming me, too. But on one occasion when we were at a party in someone's house and found ourselves in a bedroom, it was not Mr Gavin who warmed me, but his then girlfriend who arrived breathing fire and had been downstairs all along, unbeknown to me. I mean, I had no idea he even had a girlfriend. And at least I was still fully clothed, if a bit disillusioned, once again.

But one fantastic thing came out of all this modelling work. Because I had been a Gorgeous Girl I was invited to the Gorgeous Girls Gala at the Royal Albert Hall. All Gorgeous Girls who accepted would take part in a stage presentation during the event. Now this really did send me up to the clouds. THE ALBERT HALL. ME! ON STAGE! ONE OF THE PERFORMERS IN THE SHOW! AND BACKSTAGE! Backstage at the Albert Hall …

It's late 1963. I'm 14, and Mum and I have just moved into a house in Weston-on-the-Green with Dad and I've somehow persuaded him to drive me and my village friend Margaret Cox all the way up to London in his little Ford where we are to go to the Albert Hall and see a pop concert.

Playing at this pop concert will be The Beatles, The Rolling Stones, and several other bands which will include The Hollies, Manfred Mann and Herman's

Hermits. The Beatles are big, the Rolling Stones just coming along, having had their first chart hit. We're not that bothered with The Stones – they look a bit scruffy and they aren't all that good looking, compared with The Beatles. It's The Beatles Maggie and I want to see.

Every Saturday for the past few months we have met up in the front room of her parents' cottage, at 11 a.m. precisely, wearing our best make-up and our best clothes, and we have adorned the walls with our Beatles posters and we have played each and every Beatles track (their first LP has just been released) while dancing The Twist. We've even made Beatles badges to wear. Our Beatles Saturday Club only ever consists of Maggie and I (few other kids live in the village anyway).

So we get to the Albert Hall, giggling and nervous. Dad manages to park the car right next to Manfred Mann's van (big excitement and cue for a photo) and we run round the hall looking for the stage door.

Here! Hundreds of girls already here, some screaming. We wait and then through a large glass wall, inside the building we see five scruffy boys walk down a stairway to the left of the stage door. Someone says it's the Rolling Stones! And I look as hard as I can, and I see an ugly one with dark hair, a slightly less ugly blonde one and, waving cockily to us, a lippy one. There are two more but they are both boring and are wearing ties, so I take no notice of them at all.

I am not a fan of any of these boys really – but I scream anyway. That's what you do. You see – or maybe hear – a pop star in real life, and you scream.

Inside the hall you can't hear anything on stage for the screaming. We are sitting as you face the stage, halfway up from the stalls, halfway back from the stage on the right. Dad's there too, but he doesn't scream.

Paul McCartney's singing but you can't hear anything except the 'Yeah, yeah, yeah' bit. George, George is my favourite, he looks so sweet.

I think, as I stand there screaming though no sound is coming from my mouth now as I have screamed myself hoarse, there is no place else in the world to be at this minute except here – and here I am. Let me stay in this minute for always, God, please.

Pop music and the pop culture was my main survival method from the first time I saw Billy Fury's face on the magazine throughout my teens. Yes, there were other things I enjoyed – cats, horse riding, writing poetry, cycling – but if you had asked me what one thing I couldn't live without, it would have been pop.

In most ways I was a very ordinary teenage girl, getting through school and life as best we all could. But my boredom threshold was, perhaps, lower than many other of my schoolmates. And I often felt extremely sad and lonely. I needed to dream, I needed to plot and plan for a more exciting life, and for a world full of colour and light and laughter and people. Pop, as well as giving me a regular injection of excitement, gave me something to aspire to – for right from the age of 13 I knew that all I wanted to do was listen to pop music, and that later on, I wanted to write about the celebrities, and be part of their world. I played the piano up to grade 3 but it was never playing the music that interested me – it was all the rest.

I didn't go to a pop concert until The Pop Prom at the Albert Hall, and after that I didn't go to another one until Gene Pitney came to Oxford when I was about 15, and then not to another one until I went to see Billy Fury sing live for the first time at Leighton Buzzard a few months later. Much as I loved these concerts it wasn't totally necessary to go to them to enjoy all the excitement and fun of that world. The BBC's *Top of the Pops* and ITV's *Ready Steady Go!* every week brought it all right into our sitting room at home; *Fabulous* gave me titbits of news, and Radio Luxembourg provided a long-distance air of part-mystery, part-sharing.

Why was it so important to me? Why is it important in almost the same way to the teens of the twenty-first century? In many respects nothing has changed in fifty years. Pop was the light, pop was fun, pop demanded nothing of me but my time and devotion. Pop was slightly impersonal – you could stay uninvolved if you so wished, Billy Fury or The Beatles on the Dansette wouldn't ask you to kiss them if you didn't want to. You could worship from afar and everything would be fine.

Then if you felt like it, you could dash round after them like an innocent groupie and try to steal an autograph, a smile, a moment or two, even a hug or a peck on the cheek and you could feel special because some of the stardust was yours.

All this depended, also, upon the pop stars having – or at least making a show of having – a glamorous, desirable lifestyle. So you wanted to see the cars, the pretty girlfriends, the expensive guitars, the swish apartment, or at least to know they existed. And you wanted to know that underneath all this there was also an element of 'just like you'. So it was good to read that Billy Fury loved birdwatching and was shy or that George Harrison had lived in a grotty area of Liverpool. It made you like them all the more. And it made you think, 'Well if he did it from there, I can make something of myself too.'

And of course there was the music. In the first ten years of my life the only music I listened to was the music my family chose to listen to, either on the BBC radio or on the old gramophone. Brother Robert liked Perry Como, my sister liked Pat Boone, and my mother liked Frank Sinatra. I don't know who my Dad liked, he never said (until many years later, he announced he was a fan of Susan Maughan singing 'Bobby's Girl', but I think that must have been a single aberration). All this was pleasant but unmoving to my ears. Unimportant background to a life of horse riding and cycling. As I neared 10, you could sometimes here occasional snatches of more interesting music on the radio (it was probably early Elvis, Jerry Lee Lewis, and Bill Haley) but my parents always turned the sound down as soon as they started.

I remember clearly the first time I heard a song I truly loved on the radio. It was The Everly Brothers singing 'Cathy's Clown'. It was beautiful, it was immediate gratification, it was easy, it was pop. I was 10 years old. Shortly after that my parents split up.

Pop gave my teens brightness and excitement, and hope and oomph. Without it my life would have been dull, dull, dull, sad, sad, sad. Years later I still remember that buzz and when I see today's youngsters and teens screaming, just like I did, but at One Direction or Justin Bieber, or some other twenty-first-century equivalent of my teen heroes, I see pop is still a crucial part of life at that age.

Even now, I can't drive past the Royal Albert Hall without giving it an imaginary salute. OK, even if some of it was 100 per cent naff, I can think of worse memories to have than watching The Beatles and The Stones on the same bill at the Albert Hall.

Classical music, opera, jazz – I like some of all of those very much indeed but for me pop is king. One of the best autobiographies I've read in recent years was that by the Rolling Stone man himself, Keith Richards. In his book *Life* he told in detail of his young life and how much music meant to him, how a new life began for him when he first heard tracks by the old blues men of the USA. He may have been the ugly one with dark hair back in the day at the Albert Hall, but my goodness, if you want to know what popular music meant to us in the '50s and '60s – you'll never get a better insight than his. And he'd grown into his looks quite considerably by the next time I saw him, when I was about 22.

So you see why the Albert Hall was always a place of mystery, excitement beyond expectation, almost iconic to me. The Gorgeous Girls ball had to be one of the highlights of my year. I went to a boutique near Barkers in Kensington High Street, long since disappeared, and bought my dress – a short straight crocheted red dress and a flesh-coloured petticoat to go underneath it. A similar style of dress is right back in fashion now, but without the petticoat. I made myself up with shaking hands (it was a happy day when I finally stopped shaking enough before I went out to put my make-up on properly) and *The Daily Mirror* sent a car for me.

And I went in the stage door. That was the proudest moment of my life up until this point with the possible exception of getting the job at *Fab*. I'd imagined it all a hundred times and it wasn't much different – miles of curving corridors, wide and low, few windows, peeks through the curtains to the stage, hospitality room, chatting with some of the other Gorgeous Girls.

Looking back at the photos, I have to say the title 'Gorgeous Girl' was no great accolade, nor very accurate, as most of us were little more than ok-looking. No doubt the *Mirror* photographers had arrived at high streets all over the country on wet Saturdays looking for Gorgeous Girls to photograph. Cold, wet and wanting to get back to their women or their pubs, they'd photographed the first girl they had seen who possessed two legs, a bust, long hair and a short skirt.

Never mind, I got to meet Tom Jones. He was quite famous by this time so we all gathered round him for the photo call and after an audience was in place (who? how had they billed the event? – I have no idea, I guess Tom Jones could fill the hall though) and after a few drinks and as far as I recall no rehearsal, we were all called onstage to be announced as the Gorgeous Girl winners. We each felt like Miss World, which at the time wasn't actually a bad thing.

Not long after this, the photographer Beverley Goodway (later the most famous page-3 photographer of all time) rang the office and asked Unity if I could go and have my photo taken for the *News of the World* who were running a competition looking for Britain's Sexiest Girl and wanted me to model as an example of the kind of girl they were looking for. No doubt Beverley had chatted to his friend Kent Gavin on the *Mirror* who had passed on his old list of Gorgeous Girls, but even so, I allowed myself to be flattered.

I turned up at the studio, round the back from the offices, in black skinny-rib jumper, black hotpants and a belt, with long Biba suede boots, hair well ironed, and full warpaint (as Dad used to call it) in place. This was the first time I had done a proper studio shoot on my own with people other than the *Fab* team around so I felt nervous, but Beverley cracked some jokes and clicked away at the right moments and all thanks to him, the photo which eventually appeared made me look quite nice, considering there was no airbrushing in those days. I have a memory of him asking if I wanted to take my top off but as far as I can recall I didn't – I would have died of shame. These were (just) the days before page 3.

I also did a shoot for the *Sunday Mirror*. Again, Unity got the call from one of her cronies there asking her to send along a couple of *Fab* girls for a shoot. I went with Sue, the office junior, and up at the *Mirror* we found about six other girls in the studio and a tall, dark-haired guy whose autograph I knew I had to get. For it was Engelbert Humperdinck, my mother's idol and the top singing sensation of the day.

What we had to do was sit at his feet screaming while the pics were taken, to illustrate the idea that he was the latest heartthrob. 'Enge' was a complete flirt and obviously in his element but he wasn't my type, nor me his. I believe that one of the girls who was eventually edited out of the published photo, ended up being the lucky one, or it was certainly shaping up that way when I left the session. The photo was published on the front cover of the *Sunday Mirror* and my mum was, I think, quite impressed even though her beloved daughter looked absolutely ridiculous.

Around this time I went to a press party for Billy Fury, up at Larry Parnes' apartment on the Cromwell Road in South Kensington. I believe it was Fury's engagement party (to Judith Hall) but I could be wrong. Larry had been Billy's manager for years, while Hal Carter was, at first, his road manager, then later he took on Billy's proper personal management. At this party was a guy called Bertie Green, who was about 60, and owned a nightclub in Mayfair.

'You must be a model,' he said disingenuously.

'No' I said but went on to explain that I had done modelling for free as a sideline.

'Well you should be paid … why don't you come along to my office and we'll talk about it … I could get you plenty of modelling work. I could make you famous like Twiggy.'

Did I fancy myself as a model? It sounded like fun and glamour and money, and I fancied seeing what it was like to be famous. I spent a couple of days and nights wondering if I should give up my 'career' on *Fab*; agonising, in fact – it seemed like a tough decision at the time. Eventually I decided to just go with the flow and see what happened and off I raced to this guy's club by Berkeley Square after work one day, full of hope and ambition; it never crossing my mind to wonder how a night club owner could get me top work as a photographic model.

The club was in darkness but, as instructed, I let myself in a large windowless side door and down some stairs where Green stood, cigar in hand, fat belly (nothing else at this stage) protruding from his trousers. I realised I didn't like him, one bit, but I still followed him into his office. There seemed to be no one about at all except him but, I reasoned, it was early for clubs – not yet 7 p.m.

'So you want to do modelling. What kind of modelling do you want to do, Judy?' Green asked.

'Err – in the magazines I suppose. I don't know. What sort of modelling do you think I should do?'

'I think we should take some photos and then decide. Just leave it all to me. Look, here's a contract. You just have to sign it and I will be your manager and do the deals for you. I will make you a star. You could earn thousands of pounds a year.' To someone on less than £10 a week, that sounded rather cool.

Handing me a sheet or two of typed A4 paper he poured himself a brandy. I glanced at the paper and after a few moments the door opened and a dark-haired girl came in, dressed in sequinned bra and G-string. She was probably about 22.

'This is Simone. She is one of my dancers here. I think you two will get on,' said Green. To which I didn't know what I was expected to say, so I said nothing.

'I would like it if you two would get on. You do like girls don't you, Judy?'

'Well yes of course,' I said. 'I do like girls.'

You have to remember this was 1968 and I hardly knew that lesbians existed, least of all lipstick lesbians. My lesbian experience to date had been discussing some butch tweed-trouser-wearing women in a pub once with my sister and trying to work out why, if they didn't like blokes, they all wanted to be blokes.

So I thought Green meant, did I like girls. As friends. Full stop.

Simone shimmied her way towards me, put her arms around me and made to give me a snog. At which point I found a dexterity of foot unknown to me since winning the girls' under-12 80yd dash at Witney Grammar School in 1961, untangled myself and scarpered still holding the contract.

I shook all the way home and told no one. I vowed never to speak to Bertie Green again, but next day the phone rang at *Fab*.

'Bertie here, dear – you were late for an appointment were you, last night?' he said sarcastically. I couldn't think what to say. 'You weren't upset, were you?' he continued.

'Er – no, no.'

'Well that's good. You said you liked girls, but maybe you don't. You don't need to worry. You just be honest with Bertie. You come back to the club tonight and we'll be alright this time, okay?'

'Okay.'

So I went back – no Simone, good.

Bertie's willy hanging out – not so good.

This time he asked me to pleasure him as he stood there, in the centre of his office floor. 'There is no-one here today, Judy, except me. And I have locked the door.' His voice was menacing. I could hardly believe that my recently acquired lovely, poppy, light life full of fun and good dreams had evaporated in a second because of this man.

OK, I was probably not going to get killed. It was only a willy. And he wasn't going to rape me with it, that much was obvious, he just wanted what would now be called a blowjob. It seemed easiest to just get on with it, which is what I did. Not how I would have liked my fellatio career to begin, but there you are, one can't always make these choices.

And it didn't take long once I put my mouth to it. Not my mind – my mind was away somewhere else where the sun was out and The Herd were playing in the background. Keep him even tempered and get out of here. Which he was and I did. I didn't even cry – once he unlocked the door, I just wanted to breathe the London air, get far away and pretend it had never happened. I would not let him spoil my life, I would not.

By now, of course, I realised that my modelling career wasn't going to take off via this route at least – but Mr Green didn't give up easily. He began making what would now be called nuisance phone calls to me at the office. Luckily I hadn't given him my home address, never having filled out the contract he had shown me. Every day I would dread the phone ringing – him asking me to go round and see him, me making excuses, not wanting to say 'sod off you dirty old man' in case it angered him more.

Ring ring. 'Bertie here, my dear. Will you come round today? We can be good for each other.'

Never having been very quick-witted verbally I found it hard to think of excuses that would sound convincing enough, but I soon made sure to think some up every day just in case he rang.

He would always sign off by saying, 'Don't worry, I won't tell anyone' – thus planting in my mind the idea that of course if I didn't comply he WOULD tell. By now I was imagining that he had a gang of heavies to send round to get me and/or to make sure I never worked in this town again. (I'd probably been watching too many Westerns and gangster movies on TV.)

I'm not sure how far from the truth my imaginings were, but I felt trapped, stupid, dirty and indignant all at once. I didn't feel I could tell anyone about it because I felt it was all my own fault for being naïve. I felt ashamed, and guilty.

After a couple of weeks and a last sleepless night wondering how to get myself out of what seemed an impossible situation, I made a decision about what I would do next time he rang. When he did, I was so frightened my voice wobbled and shook and my hand was shaking so much I dropped the receiver. I had written down on a piece of paper my 'script' and I read it out to him, word for word.

'Look, Mr Green. It has been very kind of you to take an interest in me and to try to help me in my career, but I have decided I don't want to be a model. It's not for me. I want to be a journalist. I also have a new boyfriend who would prefer I don't come to see you again so I would very much appreciate it if you would not ring me any more.'

'Oh, I see, my love, I see. Well I think you're being very silly. I think you will regret it. Let me know if you change your mind.'

He disappeared, I put the phone down, ran to the toilets and threw up.

At the best of times, I was not very good on the phone – yet another of my secretarial attributes that didn't really work well for me. People would call and I couldn't hear what they said their names were, so I'd buzz through to Unity and say:

'There's a phone call for you.'

'Who is it, dear?'

'I don't know.'

'Well didn't they say?'

'Yes, but I couldn't hear.'

'Well why didn't you ask them again?'

'I did but I still couldn't hear and I didn't like to ask any more. Can't you just speak to them?'

So she would. If she was out or unavailable, people whose names I couldn't hear would leave messages for her to ring them, so Lord knows how many calls from superstars or agents with scoops she missed because of me.

And after that Green conversation, I didn't answer the phone at all for two weeks in case it was him ringing back. Every time it rang I would go to the loo. Eventually I began answering it again but if the voice at the other end sounded at all like him I'd put the phone down. One day after I'd slammed the phone down in just such a panic, it rang again and this guy said, 'WAIT WOMAN! Why did you just put the phone down on me? It's Owen. Why on earth Unity employed you I'll never know ...'

So Green nearly cost me my job but I never did hear from him again. I think he just decided I wasn't worth the bother – there must have been plenty more girls who would give him what he wanted in return for promises of modelling or dancing work. I somehow felt I'd had a hugely lucky escape – and couldn't wait to erase the worst memories of those few weeks from my mind. I'd escaped from a poor man's casting couch, and I would never make that mistake again, never.

And of course my wonderful modelling future was no more. Not that I cared. I realised that models have a short shelf life whereas hacks can go on a long, long time – and, from what I know about it, they can have much more fun – certainly if they are showbiz hacks, anyway.

My sister was shortly to leave *Honey* and Fleetway, where all the excitement and shallow living was getting too much for her, and move to the quieter, more earnest backwaters of the Oxfam organisation, but towards the end of my first year I would still sometimes wander through the maze of corridors and meet her at *Honey* to pop over to the Hoop and Grapes for a half of cider at lunchtime – which, over a period of months, transmogrified into several scotch and cokes, the trendy drink of the era.

One day as I hovered outside Ann's office waiting for her to finish talking to the editor, Audrey Slaughter, I heard the voice first – very very loud and very very cockney with almost a hint of Lloyd Grossman to it (though of course he hadn't been invented in those days).

I couldn't help but turn around to see from where this noise came. I first saw the mini-mouse legs – extremely long, extremely thin and very shapeless – beneath the hem of a miniskirt, striding towards me. The legs and the skirt were the only 'mini' things about this very giant of a person. My gaze went up – and up, and up – to find in a most shocking, revelatory, fascinating way, one of the most unattractive top halves I'd ever seen in my life. Short, mousy flat lank and greasy hair, large what looked like NHS specs and the most ginormous set of front teeth you ever did see. I couldn't find one speck of beauty in all of it but what amazed me most was the cutting edge teen fashion she wore, as if Twiggy would give up the ghost and go and work in Woolworths immediately if this person were to happen to want to take her place; as if to say 'Look at me – aren't I the best thing you've ever seen! Aren't I fab!'

She had the confidence of a female Robert Maxwell (the boss of the huge *Mirror* organisation) and the same kind of 'look at me' aura. I saw him once at the *Daily Mirror* building in Holborn, sweeping through reception to his private lift. Truly larger than life in every way so that you shuddered slightly as he walked past, were glad he'd gone but feeling the empty space left behind. Horrifying – but kind of fantastic. The original shock and awe.

Maxwell's female clone walked on by … and my sister came from her office.

I pointed down the corridor at the disappearing back of the giant.

'Do you know who that is?'

'Oh, yes, she works on *Petticoat* (*Honey*'s sister magazine for teens). I think she's in the fashion department. Her name's Janet Street-Porter.'

A completely wonderful example of how to get on in life with the sheer strength of your own self-belief. An asset that, it appears, has in the intervening years, never deserted her. Not that I'm saying she wasn't brilliantly clever and supremely talented as well – no doubt she was. Either way, though I saw her around a lot I was never to become a friend. In fact, I don't think she ever said one word directly to me, once, ever. And soon Janet left us mere mortals all behind on her path to greater, deserved things.

Many years later I shared a first-class carriage from Yorkshire to London with her, no one else in the compartment at all. And she still didn't speak to me. Nor I to her, so I can't really complain. I did think about saying, 'Oy, you – I remember you when you worked on *Petticoat* magazine!' But she had an invisible 'do not disturb' sign around her neck and I couldn't really think where the conversation would lead anyway, so silence ruled for two hours and remembering the voice, it was probably just as well.

My Yorkshire rambling friend 'fat Mick' worshipped the ground she walked on in later years – and, as president of the Ramblers Association for some long time, walked on a lot of ground she did. I've recently become a real fan of Janet because of her TV walking programmes and her superb opinionated journalism. And she's grown into her looks, no doubt about it. You see – I'm a fan again. I'd give anything to be her friend …

Anyway, back at Fleetway and a few drinks later in the pub, Janet was temporarily forgotten. It could well have been that day that I had a few too many ciders/scotches and fell down in the lift on the way back up to *Honey*. Ann had to pick me up and get me out in full view of her colleagues, and I sometimes wonder if her main reason for leaving *Honey* was to get away from me. If so, it was a wise decision as very many drunken performances by me in and around the office would follow in the next year or two. In those days, drinking too much was considered quite glamorous and, on Fleet Street, a badge of honour, not a sign of impending alcoholism.

And all this time, I was still searching and hoping for a best friend.

One girl who worked on another of the 'teen' magazines – *Valentine*, I think – in the same building seemed to want to be just that. Trish began visiting my office every day and I found her very friendly and easy to get on with. Down to earth, nothing special to look at with shoulder length mouseycoloured hair and little make-up, but attractive enough and great company. She made me feel good. We began sharing a lunch together sometimes in the Fleetway canteen – a dark and miserable place in the bowels of the building – and she would occasionally go for a quick drink after work before making her way on the buses down to where she lived with her parents in South London. Trish seemed very wordly wise although she was only a year or so older than me.

I was highly flattered and touched when one day she arrived at my desk bearing a gift – a little dolphin brooch in blue. It was very pretty.

'I wonder,' she said, 'If you'd like to come down home with me one evening and have something to eat?'

Well that sounded just great to me who hadn't seen the inside of anyone's house as a guest in what seemed like forever. So after work one day we took the long journey down to her place via various buses.

Once outside my familiar territory I found myself getting tongue tied with her and strangely apprehensive. But she plugged away and kept the chat going and eventually we arrived at her house, which was all in darkness.

'Oh sorry, forgot to tell you – my parents are away!' she explained brightly, letting us in. The idea of food seemed to have been forgotten as Trish put on the gas heater in their sitting room and invited me to sit on a cushion next to it. She then sat in front of me, unzipped my suede boots and took them off. At this point I began to feel seriously, uncomfortably, that all was not what it seemed but I couldn't work out what the problem was.

She put on some music and got us some alcohol. And there I sat, getting hotter and hotter and hotter and realising with complete dismay that my feet were smelly. And gradually she moved her cushion closer and closer and closer. And I moved my feet further and further away from her but the smell still pervaded the air in the room.

And then she invited me to take my top off 'As you must be very hot ...'

Now while I knew all about gay men, up until that point I had had little experience of lesbians apart from Simone, the lipstick lesbian, and the butch tweedy women in the pub. But even in my naivety I realised with horrible clarity that Trish was making a move on me. And I didn't like it one bit.

I have no idea what I said to her but within seconds I was up, boots back on, coat on, and off out of that door like a longdog. I have no idea how I got home, I don't remember. Why had it taken me so long to suss it out? Well I just had so wanted a friend, a proper friend.

Trish stopped coming round to the office after that and another potential friendship had melted away. Why was life so damned complicated? What was wrong with me?

Over the months I slowly enjoyed a kind of metamorphosis from country bumpkin into slightly more of a *Fab* person both outwardly and inwardly. As my hair grew very long, I began straightening it using my ironing board and iron (I would crouch over the board, spread my hair on it and iron it until I could smell burning). I also began to enjoy shopping. Not least, because, at last, my prayers had been answered. I had begun to relax a bit into my London life, had given up worrying about my friendless (and boyfriendless) state, and so I had found a friend. Or, to be more truthful, she found me.

Julie Webb came to work at *Fab* as a feature writer doing pop, and for some reason decided to take me under her wing. I still don't know why, as she had plenty of contacts, plenty of friends and guys always after her, and though she lived in Watford, she knew her way around London, the club scene and the media. She had the savvy of Trish and the looks of Simone, but no way was this girl after me in that way. How did I know? Well, easy – she liked men.

What I gave to Julie in return, I have no idea unless it was a well-deserved sense of superiority, but the fact is that she began inviting me for lunch, out for a drink – and after a few weeks of this I woke up one morning and realised that I HAD A FRIEND. Boy, it felt good. I hadn't realised quite how lonely I'd been. And just as importantly, her own fab self-confidence began rubbing off on me.

Julie initiated me into the delights of shopping in the lunch 'hour' which often stretched a bit into two or three. As the shops around Ludgate Circus and Fleet Street were sparse, mostly off-licences for the Fleet Street imbibers, and Carnaby Street was beginning to feel a bit naff, she took me to Kensington.

Isn't it strange how you do things that seem quite ordinary, normal, nothing to think about later that day, and years later you think WOW, I really did that. I bought stuff at the old Biba shop on the north side of High Street Kensington. You'd shove your way in past beautiful young women making their way out, Biba bags laden, and there was this fantastic, low-lit, full to brimming shop with clothes in colours never seen before – dusty pinks, plums, dove greys, lots of feather boas, floppy hats, velvet, felt. And the boots – knee-length suede to die for. This was heaven. And the make-up. Again, dusty, smudgy, deep colours. And the music …

The assistants were all gorgeous and beautifully dressed – this was the first shop I had ever been in where you felt jealous of the staff and slightly intimidated by their attitude. It really was the first time I'd been surrounded by cool on that level.

Another place we used to go was the old first Laura Ashley shop just round the corner from South Ken tube station. We often used to borrow clothes from there for fashion or beauty photo sessions and I remember going there with the photographer Roger Brown and picking piles of what I considered quite trendy tiny-floral pattern cotton dresses, floor-length with gathered waists and lace around the collars and neckline. What we fancied buying we got at huge discount – within months Laura Ashley was huge and within a year, had gone global.

By late summer 1968, I'd been at *Fab* over a year, and thanks mostly to Julie my social life had at last begun to exist. I hardly ever saw the inside of my bedsit in Avonmore Road, except to sleep and recuperate.

Nigel Hunter became a mate. Nigel had worked on the 'legitimate' side of the music press for several years but had been made redundant when something folded. Using his many contacts in the media and music world, one of whom was Unity Hall, he finally landed freelance work doing concert and record reviews – and writing a column for *Fab*. Undaunted by the fact that he was heading for 40, Nigel incongruously wrote the fictional diary of a teenage boy called Ross, managing to garner a large following of Ross-loving *Fab* readers over the next year or two.

Divorced as he was, he began squiring me, in the most gentlemanly fashion, to various press parties and fab events all over the capital. We were never 'an item', and so for the first time in my life I had a great non-threatening, non-sexual, friendship with a hetero man AND a great non-threatening, non-sexual friendship with a hetero woman.

Weekends were often still a quiet time for me. I'd sometimes head to Buckingham to visit my mother, and very occasionally I would go to Littlemore in Oxford to see my dad, where he lived with his new wife, Audrey – but those visits came to a halt when I realised I was causing a rift between them. I was in bed one morning when I heard her give him a list of things that were wrong with me, from the appalling length of my skirts (too short) and hair (too long), to my false eyelashes, my panstick make-up and my taste in music. She was an ex-schoolteacher and more of a Betty Hale (the assistant editor) type than a Judy Wills type, for sure. So I left dad and her in peace for a few years until my skirts grew longer and she could take me along to bingo with them without any embarrassment.

Nigel lived only ten minutes' walk from me in a flat off the Holland Park Road so at weekends, when work jaunts were thin on the ground, we would meet up and have a meal or a drink. Sometimes we'd go to visit friends of his in the home counties, or get together for Sunday lunch with his mates like Rodney Burbeck, who was editor of *Music Business Weekly*, in pubs in Kensington or the West End. Then I'd have a quiet Sunday evening at the bedsit in preparation for the round of drinking thrashes in the week ahead.

I truly believe that press parties were the major cause of my almost-downfall and almost-sacking at *Fab* not long afterwards. God, there were so many of them – you could go to a pre-lunch drinks party for a new record label, a lunch launch for a new theatre show or pop band, a 6 p.m. film screening with free champagne throughout, and around 8 p.m., there would always be a band playing at some club such as the Marquee who would want Nigel, or Julie, along to get a review. Even when I was still a secretary and not a writer, no one ever minded if gatecrashers arrived, and often, anyway, the invites were for two people.

It is the truth to say that a lot of the music press (mainly composed of young male chancers) would literally have starved and been teetotal but for these thrashes. You could have easily eaten and drunk well all week on these freebies. And I can admit that I don't remember ever cooking for myself at the Avonmore Road bedsit – perhaps I'd make a sandwich or heat up a can of Heinz Tomato Soup but that was it. After two years living on my own I still could cook nothing except fish pie with hard-boiled egg – for some very peculiar reason, the only dish my mother ever taught me.

Towards the end of my first year at Fleetway, just as I was beginning to feel relaxed and comfortable with my work, the team at the magazine, my surroundings and my ability to handle myself, editor Unity announced that she was leaving to work on the *News of the World*. I was horrified. I had found her easy to work for; once you got over her quite stern expression she was a pussycat. She'd also taken to writing trashy novels in office time, which she used to get me to type out clean for her, so we had a nice reciprocal thing going – she let me do what I wanted as long as I kept on typing.

Worse! Ass Ed was getting the job. Ass Ed was the formidable assistant editor, Betty, who had spent the past months staring disapprovingly across the corridor at me from the open door of her office which looked directly onto me at Ed's Sec desk. She had undoubtedly witnessed, and probably made notes about, every one of my mistakes and indiscretions, late arrivals, long disappearances, and drunken returns after lunch.

We were diametrically opposed kinds of people. I was 19 or so, she was about 40. I had long ironed hair and miniskirts, she had short permed hair and tailored suits from Austin Reed. I wore tons of make up, she didn't wear much. I was late into the office more than was good, she was never late. I drank scotch and coke, or cider, every day; she drank wait wain (as she pronounced white wine) occasionally, with food. I lived in a tacky bedsit in West London; she lived in Radlett, Hertfordshire – spiritual home of the middle-aged and what would now be called Middle England.

I liked boys and flirting. Betty was married to Eric, her long-standing husband who disapproved, I believe, of the frivolous nature of *Fab*, its staff, its readers and its whole *raison d'être*. Well if he didn't he always looked as if he did. He was a fair bit older than her, with glasses, suits, grey hair. As you can imagine, he, too, disapproved of me, or always looked as if he did. What Betty was actually doing working for *Fab*, no-one was ever too sure. But there she was.

So to know she was going to be editor put fear into me, as well it might. Things were going to change around here – if she didn't say it, she might as well have done.

About the time Betty was promoted, I seemed to be appearing in the papers but was not a huge way down the road to my ambition of being a writer. I would do tiny bits for the news page and I was responsible for the Readers Write section (the letters page), and also gave Betty a couple of rather strange Patience Strong rip-off poems I'd written. She decided to use them as captions to go with large dreamy photos of a couple of celebrities. I think the first words I ever had published in *Fab* were a short, corny poem to accompany a fey picture of Donovan, Britain's answer to Bob Dylan. Not sure what the *Fab* readers made of that but I expect my mother liked it. Apart from that, my writing career wasn't exactly taking off.

Amazingly, not long after Betty was promoted to editor, she promoted me to beauty editor. It was only later that I found out why, but that's another story.

Now beauty editor may not sound like much to you – but it was a start.

four

Something Groovy and Good

1969

Lulu's tied for first at the Eurovision song contest with 'Boom Bang-a-Bang' and she's married Maurice Gibb. *Midnight Cowboy* wins best film at the Oscars. Nixon's president. The Beatles are all but finished. Paul McCartney's married Linda, John's married Yoko, George has been busted, and Jim Morrison of The Doors has been arrested for being drunk. Drunk?

Being a beauty editor turned out to be incredibly boring most of the time. Meeting cosmetic company PRs, writing about ten different shades of lipstick. To perk the job up a little I got readers involved, doing some of the first 'before and after' makeovers you are ever likely to have seen. When I could, I also got small-time female celebs involved. Lesley Ann Down, who had just been voted face of the year or similar, agreed to a session then didn't turn up. Kiki Dee agreed to it then rang me to say she wasn't confident about her looks and didn't know what to do about her hair, which she hated. In other words, she could have done with some hair and make up advice, but couldn't cope with the trauma. I kind of understood that.

For an occasional scive, Roger Brown or one of the other photographers and I would go off on a location shoot. These were sometimes quite amusing. I would try to persuade some C- or D-list actress or pop singer to be our location model. Liza Goddard, who found huge fame shortly afterwards on TV in *Take Three Girls*, agreed to one of these. We picked her up from her bedsit in North London somewhere and she was incredibly charming in a loudish, poshish way. Poor girl didn't realise what we had lined up for her – a day posing in a lake (yes, *in* the lake, not near it, or on it) in Surrey somewhere and she never forgave me. It was much colder than I'd realised. By the end of the day she was inwardly spitting fire and dripping freezing algae-ridden pond/pong water and trying not to show either.

Not long after, I bumped into her in the bar at Rules restaurant in Covent Garden and she pretended she didn't remember me but she did, oh she did. I could tell by the slight panic on her face that what she didn't want was me regaling her new influential companions with the story of the day that she was so desperate for publicity that she waded waist-deep for hours through stinking hypothermia-inducing water. I can't actually remember the point of the photo, can't see what it had to do with beauty but there you are. Perhaps I just wanted to be cruel, and/or prove to myself that I at last had a bit of clout. Those were the first of the days when fashion and beauty editors would go off and photograph a model up a pyramid in Egypt just because you could, even though the skirt or the blusher you'd gone to photograph didn't even show.

Using diversionary tactics like this I just managed to keep the boredom under control. Tagging along with Julie Webb to music press parties at lunchtimes and in the evenings helped, as did frequent visits to the Hoop and Grapes where there were always a few *Daily Express* or *Mirror* hacks to be found, a photographer or two and various other members of the staff of *Fab*, notably John Fearn and all the members of the art department including Tom, whose real name was Brian.

One evening I found myself (I say 'found myself' because half the time there was no real intention on my part of doing what I did, it just kind of happened) at a private party held by the film actor Richard Harris, at his central London home. The place was packed with famous faces, famous bodies too, and drink. His wife (soon to be ex-wife) Elizabeth was there, and his young son, Damian, no doubt unable to sleep for the noise, arrived in our midst towards the end of the evening. But Harris, whose movie *A Man Called Horse* had just been released, was a fabulous host; the place was wonderful, I felt like I was finally in with the 'in crowd' and I thoroughly enjoyed myself.

I was also thoroughly enjoying stringing a few guys along, having finally more or less got the hang of having a chat and a laugh with the opposite sex in a fairly normal, non-offputting way, with only occasional lapses if someone was really fab. One night I went out with three – one for drinks after work, another took me out from my bedsit for a meal and when I got rid of him, another came round to take me to a club. Can't remember who any of them were but I do remember recounting this story with great glee to Julie, my sister, my mother and any other female who would listen. God knows why, it wasn't really something to be proud of but it was such a huge novelty to realise that at last guys were beginning to queue up. After years in the man wilderness it was quite heady and, obviously, had gone to my head.

Being friends with Julie was definitely a good thing, man-wise. She was slim and sexy looking with a good bust, big brown eyes, an excellent way with make-up and long hair (or sometimes hairpieces) that changed shade every couple of months. We both always wore miniskirts or hotpants with boots and as we both worked on teen mags it was easy to work out why would-be pop stars, DJs, and various other celeb hangers on and media people would be interested. Julie could talk to everyone and never seemed crippled with shyness, as I still was from time to time.

Noel Edmonds, who, after a spell at Luxy, had just got his big break on Radio 1, would arrive at the Hoop and Grapes to buy us a drink. It was Julie he fancied, not me, but I didn't care because in those days he wore a bright fake tan, coiffed long locks that looked highlighted even if they weren't and just loved himself, really. Nothing's changed. So for me, who couldn't stand overconfident men who fancied themselves, that just wouldn't do.

Dave Cash, who, with Kenny Everett, was another DJ on the way up, liked to drive me around London in his open-top car, which I thought at the time was an E-type Jag. Now I know different (you'll find out how if you get to the end), but anyway it was a Very Posh Car. His favourite port of call was the swish Dunhill shop in the West End, where he would buy fancy cigars and lighters. I wouldn't go in because I found the entrance too intimidating. He was a great bloke, but we didn't really click, so that eventually petered out and we never actually went on a real evening date.

Around this time, Fleetway Publications and Radio Luxembourg decided that Luxy and *Fab* should join forces, and suddenly *Fabulous* became *Fab 208*, the official magazine of the 'station of the stars'.

After that we were inundated with Luxy DJs when they were in town (they spent most of their time holed up in Luxembourg, of course). One day in the spring of 1969, a tall, slim, blonde-on-blonde boy arrived in reception, looking like a gangly sixth former. You just had to speak to him and he blushed bright red. Turned out he was only 18 and had just got off the plane from the wilds of Canada (well, Vancouver, actually) where he lived. I could immediately see why he had earned the nickname 'Kid' – it was David Jensen who somehow overcame his crippling shyness and, after a stint of several years at 208, went on to become one of the most popular radio DJs ever.

That day, we walked together to the tube station and said goodbye. Somehow he had 'got' to me – for the first time, aged 19, I felt a bit motherly towards a guy who wasn't a singer or actor. And I also had an unfamiliar and rather disquieting sensation of butterflies in my stomach. Anyway, when the Kid had gone I had this feeling that it would be very nice to see him again. I think I recognised in him a male version of me – another feel the fear and do it anyway fan, except he must have felt more fear than me as he'd come all the way from British Columbia whereas I'd caught the coach up the A40 from Oxford.

Around this time, all manner of pop people would arrive in the office, often with no warning. I can't quite see One Direction arriving at *Heat* magazine unannounced today, but in those days that's what everyone – even quite big stars – did. Most of the writers on *Fab* all shared one large office so whoever came in, we all had to put up with it – but more often than not, the visitors were no annoyance but the best part of the day.

One afternoon when I hadn't been at *Fab* long, I was sitting smoking a fag, drinking a coffee and feeling slightly bored with doing the books for the freelance payments (the part of my secretarial duties that I hated the most and used to put off until irate freelancers would ring up demanding to know where their money was) when a rather pale, sickly looking young boy with mousy, straggly hair appeared in the room accompanied by an older, more together-looking guy who was obviously his manager.

The boy was very thin, quite small and when he smiled at me, a nervous little smile, I noticed that his teeth were very strange and his eyes seemed to be mismatched. They'd come to plug him as a singer. I thought, well if this boy makes it as a pop star, I will be extremely amazed.

Anyway we all got chatting, the manager, Ken Pitt, persuaded us to put the vinyl on our record player (I believe it was a song called 'Love You Till Tuesday') and the boy perked up at the sound of his single. Yes, it wasn't bad, it was a funky ballad – we danced around the office and the little boy joined in. When it finished we all had a drink, more chat, and after half an hour or so, they left.

'Who was that?' I asked – having as usual missed out on the introductions.

'David Bowie? New boy from Kent?' says Julie.

'Well I wonder where he got him from … he's not going to go far is he? He's just not star material,' says I, and that was the first of quite a long line of miscalculations on my part about the career prospects of a variety of stars. I was certainly no Mystic Meg.

But honestly, you would never have thought …

Towards the end of my first year at *Fab*, the pop group of the moment – The Herd – were given the job of 'editing' the magazine one week so they spent quite a lot of time in the offices. I've still got an old issue of *Fab,* the cover of which is a series of twelve photos of The Herd 'editing' the magazine, and in one, I am there with Sue the office junior and Gary

Taylor, one of the band members. The Herd's lead singer was 16-year-old Peter Frampton, 'The Face of '68', who soon left them to form a more legitimate band, Humble Pie, with Steve Marriott, ex-Small Faces.

By 1969 I had two out of a maximum of three official warnings about lateness in the mornings, lateness of copy etc. Betty and I had a meeting at which she laid on the line that if I had one more warning I was out, so I promised to improve.

I tried up to a point to comply but eventually skipped off work for the day with a monumental hangover. That evening I was at 35 Avonmore Road when Mrs Filipinski shouted up the two flights of stairs to me.

'There's a phone call for you'.

So I crawled down the stairs to the hall phone and before I had even got it to my ear I could hear high-pitched ranting of which I could make out bits along the lines of: '... been today ... you're not ill ... how dare you ... last chance ... let me down ... copy always late ... you always late ...'.

It was Betty. The first and last time she ever phoned me at home, it was that serious.

As I didn't dare put the phone down on her I stood there half listening to it all until she had finished – and by the time she had finished, I was actually crying. What she said had upset me because I knew that it was all correct; that I had let her down in a big way. I wasn't so much crying for the loss of the job but because it was my own fault. It sounds stupid but until she actually told me to my face how bad I was being, I hadn't realised. In those moments I felt my early youth ending and second-stage youth beginning.

She ended the conversation with a curt, 'Come in and see me in the morning.' This, you recall, after I'd already used up all my warnings so I knew I was out.

Next day I pulled myself together to go in and face her in the office where I had taken so much crap dictation in the past.

Realising I would have to go a long, long way to find another job that held so much scope for fun and amusement, and realising that turning up at 10 a.m. and working for about five hours a day in between freebies of various kinds was a small price to pay, I felt crushed. I really, really didn't want to lose this job.

'Do you know why I gave you the job of beauty editor?' she began.

'Er, no.'

'It was because you were the worst secretary I have ever had,' she began. There was a long pause. I stared at the floor. My legs felt like jelly and I wanted to go to the loo – I had never had the sack before, well it was my first job so I suppose that was why, but I had never been in trouble before like this. At school I had been a goodie goodie, hated being told off. This reminded me of being in the headmaster's office and being given the only detention I ever got, but much worse.

'I didn't want you as my secretary any more. So I decided to give you a chance as beauty editor.'

Ah! Truth will out! And I had thought it was because of my natural and wonderful writing talent.

'And while your copy as beauty editor is good, your behaviour in all other respects, particularly your lateness in the mornings and your lateness of delivering copy, has been more than poor.

'I believe that you are now behaving like you are because you find being a beauty editor boring,' she continued. How right she was. Was it so obvious? This was her cue to say the 'sack' word.

'And so I am going to give you one last chance on this magazine.'

WHAT?

'I am going to give you a job as a part-time feature writer as well as your beauty. You have three months to prove to me that you can be a responsible member of staff here. Right, off you go.'

WOW, double WOW! Job saved *and* an end to bloody beauty in sight. From that day on, I had a great deal of respect for, and gratitude towards, Betty and I don't believe I ever let her down again. I began taking some responsibility for myself and my work and began suggesting features and turning into a Proper Person. I was never going to be a Betty Hale clone but I could at last see things from her point of view and as she'd given me so many chances I didn't want to let her down.

As it turned out, I continued doing a few beauty features for quite a while longer, right up until 1971. But at last I could do some 'proper' writing and interview some celebs.

And so not long afterwards, John Fearn, who'd been promoted to Ass Ed, told me who my first celeb interview was to be: Jim Dale. Jim had been, and still was, a huge

hit in the Carry On films and was trying to make his name
in other roles and in theatre and music. I still today have
a recording of Jim's with his own spectacular version of
Des O Connor's 'Dick a Dum Dum' on it. Now that must be
worth a few pennies.

Anyway I was delighted that my breaking-in was to be
with Jim, whose on-screen jovial-chap persona led me to
assume that he would be just as nice in real life, so as I
made my way to his home I wasn't as nervous as I might
have been.

I was to get to his house in the Pembridge Villas area
of Notting Hill to interview him on 23 July 1969. I went
there on the tube clutching my *A–Z*, found his street and
was just about to turn into the entrance to his very large
semi-detached house when behind me I heard a big engine
roaring up the road. I stepped back as the cause of this row
veered wildly into the short driveway of Jim's front garden
and then proceeded to continue across towards the front
steps and crashed into three large dustbins. Steaming, the
pristine Jaguar came to a halt amidst the most tremendous
din of metal bins and lids rolling and flying and careering
everywhere. And out of the driving seat leapt Jim Dale.
Grinning wildly but sheepishly. 'You must be Judy – sorry
about that. I didn't want to be late …'.

Despite the fact that he must have been worried about
what damage he'd done to the car (and I am sure there was
some) gentleman Jim gave me the most easy time for my
first interview. He must have seen I was inexperienced and

I've been so grateful to him ever since, and of course madly in love with him because you can't beat a combination of charm, self-effacement, good looks and intelligence coupled with – as I had witnessed first hand – a dash of recklessness in a man. He *was* sex on legs ... who'd have thought it? Pity he was yet another married man – way out of my league though, married or not.

I got back to the office, floating at the amazing delight at having spent an hour or two talking person to person with a real celeb, and began writing up the piece straight away, beginning, of course, with Jim's spectacular entrance. It made the perfect opening and if the feature wasn't called Carry on Crashing then it should have been.

However I soon found that turning an interview into a coherent feature wasn't quite as easy as I had presumed, and that one-pager took me days of pencil sucking and agony until I considered it good enough to hand in. The feature appeared a few weeks later and I don't think I've ever been as proud of anything connected with work, before or after. It had been fun to get my picture in the papers and magazines – but to get your name at the bottom of an article – now that was truly *Fab*.

Luckily, my writing speed gradually increased with my output but I can still picture myself in that Avonmore Road bedsit, with my old picnic table set up and an ancient portable typewriter on it with some A4 paper and carbon – honing my silly little pieces for *Fab* as if they were literature, late into the night.

Here's how it went:

ONE: Transcribe and type up all the shorthand notes (never anything less than traumatic – you will recall that my shorthand was the first thing to go under pressure, and my early interviews were all done using just shorthand. It wasn't until later that we were all advised to buy portable tape recorders).

TWO: Take the paper out of the typewriter and cut out all the quotes individually with my nail scissors.

THREE: Lay the quotes all out on the bed, then put a new piece of paper in the typewriter and type out a rough order to the feature in one-line ideas, with big spaces between each. Get paper out of typewriter.

FOUR: Slot the quotes into the various most likely places they might go within the feature, then when happy, sellotape them in place.

FIVE: With yet another piece of paper in the typewriter, type the whole thing out as draft copy, then remove it and go through it with a pen, making any final adjustments.

SIX: Type it all out clean.

It was a long time before I felt confident to write up an interview without this technique, and the worst scenario was if I ran out of sellotape after the shops were shut.

In later years, when I worked for a while as a freelance writer doing day shifts at the *Daily Mail*, turning out 1,000 word features on subjects I knew little about, from scratch, in an hour, including getting people on the phone for quotes, I would look back at my actual 'cut and paste' period and smile.

My features were very rarely returned to me to rewrite or do any work on, but it was laborious long hours after midnight rather than natural talent, I fear, that helped them into print for the first year or so.

I'm 14. I'm at school. It's Careers Day – when we all troop, in alphabetical order, in to see the careers master to discuss What we Want to Be When we Grow Up. This is, in theory, so that we can match our choice of O levels to our aspirations.

My turn. All I want to do is be a journalist. A writer. On a magazine.

'DO you know what you want to do, Judith?'

'Yes – I want to be a journalist. On a magazine.'

Silence for a few seconds. Probably doesn't help that my name begins with W, he's no doubt had a dreadful and long day by now.

'Well, I really don't think you're going to be able to do that. That's more the kind of career for a man. There's not much scope for you in that direction.'

'Oh, but …'

'Why not think about being a typist? Here …'

He hands me a small sheaf of info on how to be a typist or a secretary and what opportunities there are in the factories around Oxfordshire for this great career, and I'm dismissed.

And I'm *not* crushed by him. My fight-back mechanism comes in. I am even more determined to be a journalist now. There's nothing better than someone telling you you can't do something; it makes you ten times more determined. You just have to go and do it to prove them wrong.

So I have to thank that careers guy almost as much as my sister, Unity and Betty – the three people who helped me along in more positive ways. He helped me by default – but it doesn't matter where you get your motivation from, as long as you get it.

LATE 1969

Around this time we left the offices in New Fleetway and made the short move to much more dingy Old Fleetway next door. I began sharing an office with Georgina Mells who had arrived at *Fab* straight from Cardiff University and reminded me heavily of myself when I first got to Fleetway, in that she wasn't cool, hip or gorgeous to look at. But she was much more intellectual and much more self-possessed than I had been – and much, much more posh. It seemed like she'd turned the wrong way out of the lift by mistake and should really have been working at *Country Life*.

Like me, she soon learnt how to alter her appearance via miniskirts, make-up and a bit of a diet to morph into a real *Fab* person, and she quickly launched herself into the life of a budding *Fab* writer – sharing beauty and other duties with me – with all the trappings, and we began a friendship and shared adventure that lasted several years.

Around this time Julie was promoted to chief writer on *Rave* magazine, which although it was only down the corridor could have been miles away. It was a slightly more serious, 'in-depth' magazine, a monthly, and Julie began spending more time with the writers on the *New Musical Express* – for whom she eventually ended up working – leaving us poor little pop mag people behind except when she would come down and tell us all about who she'd met.

She was very possessive about her stars. She would preface their names with the word 'my', as in 'My Status Quo', 'My Showaddywaddy,' 'My Neil Diamond', 'My Slade'… but Georgina and I fought back when Edison Lighthouse came along in 1970. They had one massive hit called 'Love Grows Where My Rosemary Grows'. Sweet boys – Georgina fancied George who I believe was the drummer, while I liked the tall blonde lead singer whose name was Ray Dorey. Julie had eyes for Ray too and when she began calling the band 'My Edison Lighthouse' I felt panic and fear.

She scored points off me when they were supposed to meet up with me at a pub for an interview and they all arrived minus blonde boy. She had detained him with a promise of a bigger interview and photo in *Rave*. I was near tears relating this to Georgina, who took pity on me and plotted a new interview a couple of weeks later on another pretext. We both went along and blonde boy was there in all his gorgeousness, as was George. After the interview Georgina, who had a grand flat in a mansion block in West Hampstead bought for her by her parents, invited the whole band back to her place for tea.

Thus it was that we and Edison Lighthouse, who had been at number one for several weeks by this time and on *Top of the Pops* every week too, took the Northern Line in the rush hour. One or two commuters may have recognised them but luckily most teenyboppers would have been back home after school doing their homework. It just wouldn't have happened with a number one band of today, who, so I'm told, usually arrive with PRs, managers, stylists and hangers on, and would think you were completely bonkers if you suggested they get on the tube and pop over for a cuppa at your place.

Back at Georgina's pad we made them cheese sandwiches, gave them tea and played a few tunes on her hi-fi. It didn't work out well for me and the blonde one – it was yet another case of him being quiet and shy, and me being too overcome to do anything but watch as, replete with Hovis and Tetleys, he disappeared off back down the underground to wherever he lived. I believe Georgina had a bit more luck with George but, reticent for once, she didn't divulge too many details.

We shared the beauty features and interviews more or less randomly – pop, TV, films – and often both turned up together if we felt like it.

Occasionally other perks came along – and it was at the grand old age of 20 that I had my first flight in a plane. A freebie had come in for Heather Kirby, who was still the fashion editor, and she decided to let me have it – a trip to visit a factory in Northern Ireland. (You can see why she let me have it.)

Well, okay, it wasn't the most interesting of actual visits but I can vividly remember the huge excitement of travelling to Heathrow, boarding the little plane, being given a window seat and watching spellbound as we took off and headed up into the clouds. It rained non-stop during my few hours at a plant somewhere to the west of Belfast in the middle of Irish nowhere, but I didn't care … at last I had been off the land or sea for the first time in my life, I had been in the air. I had looked down on the land from an aeroplane. I felt great, I felt free. And I hadn't even paid for it!

For a so-called glamorous pop magazine, *Fab* didn't have its fair share of male talent working in the office. There was John, the little letters page boy, but he was about 17 and looked it. Phil from the art department was quite nice to look at but stroppy. John Fearn was a smashing guy but with his bowtie and glasses, he always reminded me of the old TV star, Harry Worth. But most of the staff were female.

So one day when a new sub-editor arrived, and he was tall and slim and definitely under 30, most of us were quite thrilled, especially Betty, who had obviously employed him as much for his testosterone as his ability to spot typos. His name was Richard, and she was so enthused that she devoted a large part of that week's Ed's Letter to his arrival.

Unfortunately, his sharp sub's eye didn't extend to that first Ed's Letter. When the issue was published, Betty's missive read something like, 'This is a great week – we have something new up here. Six foot of dark, handsome dick…'.

'Dick', whose actual name was Richard Girling, never did quite live that one down. He was an unassuming, quite intense young man from Hertfordshire and we had a mild flirtation for a few weeks which culminated in me heading to St Albans with him one evening for a walk around the historic sights (he was that kind of a guy). But I didn't really fancy him that much and when I found out that he had a girlfriend in Hertfordshire whose name was Rose, that was the end of that.

By now I had met Gordon Coxhill, a young writer on the *NME*. He took a fancy to me and for a year or more pursued me quite hard. Sadly although he was a lovely guy, I didn't fancy him in the slightest. So I spent the year trying to juggle being nice enough to him so that he would invite me along on some of the (much higher-class) freebies that came his way, courtesy of the country's most respected music journal with a circulation of over 250,000 (and proudly described on its cover as a 'newspaper'), but not so nice that he got the 'wrong idea' – the phrase used in those days for a guy who thought you wanted sex when you didn't.

I would sometimes accompany him to interview stars – there was the occasion when we went to Blackpool to 'do' Cilla Black and The Walker Brothers – then attended a posh dinner with Cilla after her show. At the time both acts were huge and it was always fun to observe the stars off-duty, and after a few drinks. Even if journalists were present, if it was a private occasion everything that was said was always off the record, and this rule was never broken. Cilla liked to act the star even when she was off-duty and visibly riled if she wasn't the centre of attention at all times, but she had a great sense of fun and some fantastic tales.

The next morning, still in Blackpool, Gordon and I took a trip to the top of the Blackpool Tower, where I bought a postcard and sent it to my mum, posting it in the postbox that was provided up there. When I got back to London a day or two later, my mother rang Avonmore Road in a panic.

'Is it true?' she said.

'Is what true?' I asked her, mystified.

'Well I just got this postcard from you, saying you got married to Gordon Coxhill in Blackpool!'

'Oh' I said, 'That. No, Mum, of course I didn't. Sorry, only joking.'

Truth was, I had no recollection at all of having written that on the postcard.

Must have started on the Scotch and cokes early that day …

It was Gordon who accompanied me to Hal Carter's baby Warren's christening too, in July 1969. The photo of that day shows me, Gordon, Jimmy Campbell, Billy Fury and Judith Hall, whom he had married in May 1969, along with Hal and Sam. The relationships between us all were complicated. There was Gordon, who fancied me but I didn't fancy him; Jimmy, who might have fancied me a bit for a few minutes but certainly didn't now, but I still fancied him; and Billy, who had never fancied me and who I had fancied for years but had given up fancying through necessity. And there were Hal and Sam, the stars of the day with their baby, who knew little of all this (I hope), both of whom were lovely people whose friendship I valued with or without the added bonus of Hal's ever-growing stable of handsome singers.

Every other day there seemed to be a film screening at one of the private viewing rooms belonging to the big film companies of the day – most of these, such as 20th Century Fox, MGM and Paramount, were in or around Wardour Street, Soho. I hit upon the idea of getting a celeb to come along with me to a screening to review the films for the magazine, and the first film this worked with was *Midnight Cowboy*, relased in the UK in early 1970.

At the time the actor John Alderton was big news – he had been starring in the TV comedy series about a secondary school, *Please Sir*, which was top of the ratings and adored by *Fab* readers, of course because of the subject matter and the large coterie of young actors and actresses in the show.

To my amazement, he agreed to come along to the evening screening. Then a day or two later his agent rang and asked if John could bring somebody with him. I fixed this, wondering why he would want to bring someone else.

I'd arranged to meet him outside the screening in the West End and when he arrived, with a young lady at his side, things began to click. It was none other than Penny Spencer, the young actress who played one of the lead pupils in the series, the sexy young miniskirted girl who always flirted with 'Sir'.

They sat more interested in watching each other than the movie and at the end Alderton asked if I could ring him the next day to get his comments on the film – he could hardly wait to get rid of me. I watched as they walked away down the street, hand in hand.

Of course, John was married to the actress Pauline Collins (still is, I believe) – the two of them were one of the most famous showbiz couples of the time. I never said or wrote a word about John's friendship with Penny. It was none of my business. And maybe it was all totally innocent anyway … but I rang him next day to get the quotes and, as I had suspected, I didn't get a great deal out of him. I invented most of his review – and he certainly never complained.

In December of 1969 I was invited to my first film premiere – which included a pass to the official private reception and after-show party. This was *The Magic Christian*, a film starring Ringo Starr, who was trying to find a niche for himself in the post-Beatle world, and Peter Sellers. As Sellers was *as-close-as-this* to Princess Margaret at the time, although I didn't know that then, it was hardly surprising that she and Anthony Armstrong-Jones, Lord Snowdon, were the guests of honour.

Luckily the premiere was just down the road from my bedsit, at the Odeon on Kensington High Street. But even so, wearing a new black velvet dress, chosen for me by Julie Webb from a small boutique near Ludgate Circus (Julie also had to lend me the money to pay for it, £16, a lot of money in those days) and my high heels, I wasn't going to walk there. Oh, no.

The film company sent a limo for me and thus it was that I walked up the red carpet, heart pounding, with all the spectators going, 'Who's she? Who's she?' – in my mind at least. A few flashbulbs did pop and for an evening I lived the life of a real film star, enjoying every second.

Well, the film was rubbish but that didn't really matter.

By the end of 1969 I was getting to do more and more show business interviews as Betty's faith in my writing and interviewing abilities grew.

The best interviews were when you had to go to people's houses, as it was much more fun than impersonal hotels. I visited Mark Lester, star of *Oliver!*, at his home in Richmond, went to Yorkshire to meet Dave Bradley, star of the bird movie *Kes*, and Rodney Bewes – star of *The likely Lads* on TV, whom I found delightful, funny and unassuming – at his house in Fulham, and later at the BBC rehearsal rooms in West London. I wrote up this piece in the form of a letter to Rodney, and a few weeks later received a note from his mother, thanking me for the feature and saying how much she had enjoyed it. Sweet – another thing that would be unlikely to happen today.

Other good places to meet stars were the London pubs – things always got interesting after a drink or two. The pub (often the Coach and Horses in Greek Street) was always the meeting place when you were seeing Status Quo (Francis Rossi still owes me a fiver) or Rick Wakeman. And sometimes we went to film or TV sets, which again was good because you never quite knew what would happen – or who you would see.

One of my early visits to a set was to Pinewood Studios to interview Michael York, making what turned out to be pretty much a turkey of a movie called *Zeppelin*, along with a raft of 'English' actors including Anton Diffring, Marius Goring and Rupert Davies. While I waited on the studio floor for

York to finish being lit for a scene during a thunderstorm, I was aware of someone beside me watching the proceedings – and almost fell over when I realised it was Bette Davis, the Hollywood veteran with the piercing eyes. And now she was staring at *me*.

This was the person described by Marilyn Monroe as 'a mean old broad', and her fellow actress on *All About Eve* Celeste Holm said of her, 'she was rude … so constantly rude.'.

When you've grown up watching a true legend of the screen in the movies and on the TV – one of your own mother's ultimate screen icons – and when you suspect that they are probably ferocious in real life, it is quite unnerving to find yourself, with no prior knowledge or warning, standing in front of that person, not least when that person is giving you her trademark brand of bug-eyed stare.

Someone – probably the film PR – came to my rescue and did the introductions and much to my amazement Davis, who would have been in her early 60s, didn't eat me or turn me to stone but was very pleasant. She was one of the few actors I ever interviewed who showed any interest in someone other than herself, and was not only willing to talk to me but almost anxious to keep me chatting, was the feeling I got. Why, I'm not sure.

Anyway, I came away with more interesting words from Bette Davis than I got from Michael York, that was for certain. She had unconventional looks, but had real charm, if a bit too intensely dished out. I had only once before been gazed at in quite such an intimate way by a woman – my friend Trish back at the office who turned out to be gay. So what of her reputation as rude and mean? I have no idea – but Celeste Holm's remark that perhaps Davis's rudeness 'was to do with sex' might have been near the mark.

I did wonder what on earth she was doing there as she wasn't in that particular movie. She had made a film recently at Pinewood, called *Connecting Rooms* (another turkey – Pinewood was quite good at those at the time, it seems) so perhaps she was back to do retakes or something.

Another set I visited, in December '69, was *Coronation Street* in Manchester, where I interviewed Neville Buswell who, at the time, was playing Deirdre's partner. He was rather boring but the whole day was very fab – round every corner you'd bump into one of those so-familiar faces. I was invited into Ken Barlow's dressing room, where Ken was in residence, and happily gave me intricate details of his life and times to the point where I really, really, wanted to run away.

I also watched the filming of an episode. I marvelled at how hard the cast worked and how they all seemed to get it right in virtually one take. But Neville soon put me right on the reason why – if they didn't do scenes in a take, the day's work would run over and they could be arriving home at midnight, have to learn their lines and be back at work at the crack of dawn next day. So anyone who messed up got a right rollocking from the other cast members, and if they did it too often, calling for expensive overtime for the crew, they'd get the sack. At least that's what Neville told me.

A different journey to Manchester around the same time involved a lunch date with one of the most famous young men in the UK – George Best. George had 'written' a column for *Fab* for some time (in fact submitted by his then manager whose name was, I believe, Ken Brown). He was the first footballer ever to get the teenyboppers excited that way and no footballer since, not even David Beckham, has had the same effect, *en masse*, on girls.

The manager decided – perhaps to ensure that the column continued for another year – to invite Betty up to Manchester and, knowing that the one thing that kept George happy was the female form (especially if under 25, dressed in hotpants or a miniskirt and with long hair) asked her to bring along someone suitable. That person was me.

Not being a great football fan – and at the time having other things on my mind – I boarded the train to Manchester with her feeling not at all excited. Yes, I had clocked George on the TV but I had mainly noted that he had weedy, bandy legs, and was obviously quite short. Betty worried much of the way up that George would, in fact, not turn up at all – he always had a reputation for being unreliable.

We were to meet at the Piccadilly Hotel. And indeed he did turn up, trailing in respectful and shy manner behind Ken, almost like a toddler hiding behind his mother's skirts – something I knew a lot about.

And that was how he was, for most of our lunch. My own powers of thought and speech virtually deserted me as Ken and Betty chatted about nothing much (she was no football buff, either). After a few minutes enquiring about his new architect-designed home in Cheshire and getting just one-word answers, I racked my head to try to think of something, anything, to say to George Best that would interest him, open him up, make him laugh … but no, it was a bit like trying to get a can of sardines open – in the end you give up and find something better to eat. I amused myself by looking around the dining room and noticing that virtually everybody in there was trying hard to pretend they weren't looking at us.

It was only after downing several beers and a few chasers that George suddenly found his tongue and his sense of humour but sadly this was at the end of the lunch. I don't think George meant to be rude or sullen – I think he really was painfully shy with strangers and we just brought out the worst in each other – and he probably had a hangover as well. Perhaps he would have chatted me up if Betty and Ken hadn't been there – but I don't think so. Maybe if I'd worn a blonde wig it would have been different but I really didn't care.

At the end of the lunch he shook my hand and said goodbye and as he did so I suddenly realised what it was about him that made so many women fall at his feet or into his bed. For the first time during lunch he looked me straight in the face. And I felt my knees buckle slightly … he had the most amazing pair of ice blue eyes I have ever seen in my life – they looked at me, with a slight hint of come-on, and, too late, I thought WOW! I wish I'd tried a bit harder ….

Well, perhaps not really. He wasn't my type nor I his but I've never forgotten those eyes and the magic there. He was a superb looking young man in the flesh, he really was – from the head up, at least. The legs may have been great with a football but they never did turn me on.

In late 1969 most of my work was still beauty and the film and TV world, but on 14 December I popped round to the Marquee to see Love Affair, a young band of boys who had just one huge hit, 'Everlasting Love'. They were no great shakes on stage, but I loved the atmosphere in the old Marquee in Wardour Street – smoky, crowded, cool, hip, lots of acquaintances around. I felt that what I really wanted to do was more music and less of the actors and screenings. They were okay to a point, but actors, by and large, were self-important bores. And I wanted to feel the beat, and be a real part of the music scene, full time.

So, after my most eventful year in London yet, at Christmas, I caught the coach from Victoria station down to Aylesbury, changing on to the bus for the last few miles to Buckingham, where my Mum and Gran would be waiting for me, to spend a quiet and, frankly, deadly dull few days, just the three of us – apart from a flying visit from Gordon Coxhill at some stage over the holiday which didn't do a great deal to cheer me up. Although I wouldn't have wanted to be on my own at Christmas I found the days in Gran's tiny parlour, watching *The Good Old Days* and the like on the black and white TV stultifyingly boring. I couldn't wait to get back on the bus and back to London; 1970, I felt, was going to be great. As it turned out, I was quite wrong.

five

Some Things Are Meant to Be

1970

Women's libbers ruin the Miss World contest. Germaine Greer publishes *The Female Eunuch*. Anne Nightingale becomes the first women DJ on BBC Radio 1. Janis Joplin is dead. The Beatles formally announce they've split.

Because *Fab* was now *Fab 208*, the writers made regular trips to Luxembourg with a photographer to get stories on all the DJs and the wonderful life they were supposed to be having out there.

In truth, the guys were bored rigid most of the time as there were few clubs, few expats and basically not a lot to do. So when we turned up it always cheered them up. There was Tony Prince, Paul Burnett, Bob Stewart, Dave Christian and of course, David 'Kid' Jensen who had quietly turned himself into one of the most popular of the DJs with the listeners.

They worked out of studios in the Villa Louvigny, an ugly building complete with tower, surrounded by parkland on the edge of Luxembourg town and I can vividly recall my first visit there. As our car, driven by Tony Prince, drew up outside the so-familiar building (from the many photos of it I had seen over the years) I felt that awed, pit-of-the-stomach feeling again, a huge excitement to be here, at *208* at last. Once inside the studios on the second floor, sitting quietly listening to Tony do a show, thinking about the millions of listeners, I once more had that 'what a great job this is' feeling. Someone was paying me to live out all the dreams I ever had as a child.

I have been given a small transistor radio for my birthday. What you do is, you go to bed quite early unless it's *Dr Kildare* night. Then you tune into medium wave 208 and spend the next couple of hours trying to keep the station in tune while you listen, enthralled, to those big, booming cheerful voices coming from Europe, introducing track after track of wondrous new music – Beatles! Stones! Acts from America – Roy Orbison, Elvis, Neil Sedaka, Ricky Nelson, The Everlys. 208 is quite the most glamorous thing ever.

The worst bits are the adverts. Sometimes you wonder if you can even put up with Horace Batchelor and finding out how to spell K E Y N S H A M, Bristol, one more time – but you do. And then just when Billy Fury comes on, the station fades and you want to throw the transistor across the room because you've missed most of it by the time the sound comes through again.

You have to listen out for mum coming upstairs and later on Veronica, Mrs Hill's daughter, will come to bed and you definitely have to turn off the trannie or she'll shout at you and rip the covers off your bed.

Because Radio Luxembourg listening was somehow illicit, fraught with danger, and hard to actually hear because of the crackling and hissing, it made it even more fantastic. It was like a secret world that I, and hundreds of thousands of other teenagers in the early '60s, shared.

Remember Radio 1 didn't start until 1967, while the offshore pirate stations such as Caroline, which had started up in 1964, mostly had reception too poor for landlocked places like Oxfordshire. Also, they avoided broadcasting during the evening out of respect for 208. So throughout my early teens – if you had a trannie and you had a bed, you had 208 to transport you to a more exciting life, and, much of the time, that was all you had.

Alan Freeman, David Jacobs, Jimmy Young, Jimmy Savile, these were the original icons on our little radios – mostly pre-recording their shows from the London headquarters at 38 Hertford Street – not that we teens knew that at the time. Out in Luxembourg in the early '70s, the next influx of boys often did DJ stints at the largest local nightclub to pass the time and earn a bit of extra money. They also quite often had formal lunches and receptions with visiting bigwigs and dignitaries from all over Europe.

It was at one such lunch on my first visit to Luxembourg, in April 1970, via the Luxy headquarters in Brussels, that I was seated next to Kid Jensen. It had been a good year or so since I'd seen him up at the office when he first arrived in London. We'd spoken on the phone a few times when I needed to interview him for a few words of copy, but he was still shy so we hardly exchanged more than a few words during the lunch.

However I did have the feeling that he liked me and I had had a couple of glasses of wine, so the devil took over towards the end of the meal and as he turned away from me to talk to someone else, I whipped his as-yet untouched dessert away and swapped it for my empty plate. When he turned back his face was a picture – all men love puddings.

'Where's my dessert?'

'You ate it, Kid.'

'I did?'

'Yes – don't you remember, you said how great it was!'

Soon I began laughing and returned his pud to him from where I'd put it under the table.

That broke the ice and I learnt a valuable lesson – a sense of humour helps in most situations. We spent the rest of my two days there together, to the slight disapproval not only of the *Fab* photographer who'd accompanied me and thought it unprofessional to cohort with the interviewees, but also of most of the other 208 DJs, with the exception of Tony Prince who encouraged us in our romance, so thank you Tony.

When my few days there were up, Kid drove me to the airport and I felt bereft when the plane took off. I guess I was in love – with an actual person, not a photo or an image on the TV – for the very first time. I got back to Avonmore Road, exhausted from hardly any sleep, and went to bed clutching the radio, with 208 on, of course. Some habits do die hard.

Trying to keep a romance going when he had to be there and I had to be in London was extremely difficult, however. Faxes hadn't been invented, let alone computers, mobiles, Skype, tweets or anything remotely similar to all we have today. We had the post and we had landlines (but I still didn't even have a phone of my own, only the landlady's communal phone downstairs).

We did talk on the phone once or twice but somehow reverted to our shy personas and these talks were less than successful. It was months later that we met again – Kid came to the UK to cover the Isle of Wight Festival, which was revered as the UK's answer to Woodstock and attracted some of the greatest names in music. This year Jimi Hendrix and The Doors were topping the bill. Betty decided I should go and cover the event.

I could hardly wait to see Kid again but when we did meet, in a large room in reception at our hotel, there was Kid, an assortment of radio hangers on, and a young blonde woman called Anne Challis who worked for Radio Luxembourg in London and whom I had met a few times before. Not only was she quite attractive, she was also sitting next to Kid and was sending distinct 'he's mine' messages across the room, or at least that's what I thought. While we waited for our rooms to be allocated, Kid stood up and came across to me. My heart started thudding. At last!

'Hi! How are you doing, Judy?!'

'Fine thanks, Kid – how are you?'

'Yes, okay – I have a note here for you.' With those few words he handed me a piece of paper, then returned to his seat. I opened the note but it wasn't from him – it was from Tony Prince and was just two names – Kid and Judy – with an arrow and heart in between the two and Tony's signature at the bottom. So Tony wanted our romance to continue – but did Kid? He wasn't exactly paying me much attention. He'd walked back to sit next to Challis and didn't seem to even glance my way. Once again my lack of confidence surfaced and instead of going across to him and showing him the little cartoon as I should have, I stayed put, stuck, in my chair. I had no idea what to do.

We were all shown to our rooms and to my horror when Kid went into his, Anne Challis followed. Devastated, I continued down to my room and cried. The next morning she stuck to him like a leech, he and I had no chance to say anything to each other, and those two days at the Isle of Wight were ruined.

I was broken-hearted, I guess. My GSOH had deserted me and I could think of no way through the toughened-glass wall that seemed to be between us. Mainly because I couldn't understand what had gone wrong, and also because my Leo-ness prevented me, as it did so often, from swallowing my pride and just making the first move. I knew Kid wasn't the sort to gloat and parade a new woman like that in front of me. Did he know what was in the note? Couldn't he see how upset I was? I wasn't to find out the answers until months later.

To ease the pain of seeing Kid around at the festival and not even being able to talk to him or hug him, I tried my first drug. Well actually that's not true. I tried my first drug because I didn't know what it was. The person who shared his joint with me was called Jim Morrison, lead singer with The Doors.

Attempting to be the professional that I was slowly becoming, despite my misery I carried on with trying to get interviews, and of course, watched as many acts as I could. The line up that year was quite fantastic with so many huge names from the world of music – apart from The Doors there were (among many others) Ten Years After, Emerson Lake and Palmer, Joni Mitchell and The Who, all of whom appeared on the Saturday, and Kris Kristofferson, Free, Donovan, the Moody Blues, Jethro Tull, Joan Baez, Leonard Cohen and Jimi Hendrix, all of whom appeared on the Sunday, the last night of the Festival.

But getting interviews wasn't quite as easy at it should have been. For one thing, I had turned into a wimp. All the bravado which was now usually in place back at Fleet Street and surrounds had vanished because here were not bubblegum popstars dying to have you interview them so that you naturally felt superior and in control, but *real* musicians, *actual* American rock idols, *huge*, huge stars – people who attracted the likes of The Beast at the *NME*, *The Times* and *Rolling Stone* to interview them. The acts and the media here were *real* cool people, man, so all my life-long old feelings of inferiority returned and I felt so far not in control and wanting to get off that island *now*, a feeling reinforced by the sniffy attitude of most present to teen magazines. But I knew I had to return to the office with some stories.

I had a backstage pass – in those days backstage at a festival was some rough grass, a couple of tents, one with alcohol and sandwiches, another for the acts to get changed in, and a couple of tiny caravans for the major stars. Well maybe not quite that bad but you get the picture. It was all very basic and of course it always rained at these events as it still does today.

At the IoW it was rarely the case that PRs fixed interviews for you (not least because nobody knew where anybody else was), you just grabbed people and started asking questions – a method of interview somewhat hampered in my case by my timidity.

So my technique was to wander round this scruffy backstage area until I found someone I vaguely recognised, then muster up the courage to approach them, or, if my nerves got the better or me, to walk away and pretend I hadn't seen them in the first place. All Saturday morning I had had very few sighting of the major stars as they didn't really get going until past lunchtime. I was beginning to worry that I really would be going home with nothing when later I spied Morrison heading towards the refreshment tent on his own. My heart started racing not because I fancied him, but through my old companion, fear. And I did it anyway – hurried, as casually as was possible, over to him, lied about what magazine I was from and asked if he would chat. Sure, sure … it was hard to keep talking because he did have the most fantastic face, eyes, hair, body … he looked like a cross between a Greek god and Christ, but better looking and nicely clean-shaven.

Because the Fleet Street people I mixed with were firmly based in alcohol for kicks, not drugs, I had little experience of drugs of any sort or what they did to people. I had no idea of the physical effects or the brain effects and I had no idea what drugs of any sort looked like, smelt like, or how you took them. Hard to believe now, but true. The stories of rampant mass drug taking by all in the press, the music business, fashion, film and so on during these years are way off the mark. Yes, it happened, but of all the people I knew during these years very few did more than the occasional puff of hash.

Despite my ignorance, I did strongly get the feeling that Jim Morrison was off with the fairies. He was aware of me but in no way on the same planet.

It didn't seem laid-back to take notes so we just talked, in the bar, as best we could between us – he was pleasant but monosyllabic in his fairy world and me also monosyllabic on planet fear trying hard to stay cool. As you may imagine the interview was about as productive as a chef in a famine, but at least I'd met him. I don't recall any hangers on, managers, whatever, being there at all. Strange. He was a big star. But I guess he did his own thing.

Anyway, he offered me a roll up and I smoked it. I smoked twenty cigarettes a day at that point but found the taste of these little homemade ones quite disgusting.

Of course it contained weed but at the time I genuinely didn't know. I also didn't know that you were meant to share a joint so I smoked most of it myself while Jim Morrison, fairly politely in the circumstances, looked on. Eventually I put the stub in a nearby ashtray whereupon he rescued it and finished it off. He wandered off soon after and later was up on stage in front of the 500,000 crowd on Afton Down, me included. Another of those moments where I had to pinch myself. Surreal.

Less than a year later he was dead.

How did I feel after the joint? Well it dulled the pain I had been feeling but also addled my brain more than alcohol had ever done and made my mouth so dry I detested the sensation. Weed or any type of cannabis just doesn't suit me and although I tried it once or twice more, I eventually decided I just was never going to be a *bona fide* pothead – and stuck with the Scotch and cokes and the wine.

The dubious effects of the joint wore off, and I was left feeling tired and strangely depressed. Because of my distracted state, I seemed to spend the whole weekend on my own although I knew I had gone there with a photographer and I knew several other people who had been on the same journey down there with me. Where they all were, I can't say, nor whether or not they managed to get back to our hotel at night, nor how. Kid Jensen had apparently vanished into thin air. There were just thousands and thousands of strangers, all of whom seemed to laugh the whole time or dance or sit, smoking. Everyone having a good time, except me. That was the biggest crowd I ever felt lonely in, that's for sure.

It was Saturday evening, with two more nights of the festival to go and no early finishes – at the IoW the music went on until morning. I was obsessed by trying to figure out where I would sleep, hoping that I would find some way back to the hotel. I have never been good at staying up all night and was often laughed at when I started clubbing with Julie Webb, when I would always be the one asleep in the corner of the Revolution – the mega hot club of the day – or wherever, at midnight. Our hotel was probably 2 to 3 miles from the festival site and I had naively assumed that there would be transport back to the hotel after the end of the concert each day, but had been told by a couple of people backstage that this was never going to happen.

No transport, nothing at all, no chance of a taxi – even if you could have called one he'd never find you in the midst of thousands of people.

Around 1 a.m., I decided to walk back – but of course there was no street lighting, and anyway I didn't know the way. So I had to abandon this attempt, and was eventually forced to opt for a sleepless night under the stars (the ones in the sky, not any of the acts), wretchedly wondering where Kid was and how he and Anne Challis were getting on.

By the second night I couldn't have cared less who was on the stage, and having managed to have a short chat with both Joni Mitchell and Donovan (chosen by me because they didn't look too scary; I had used up all my bravado on Jim Morrison), had also given up on trying to find interviewees. By this time I had managed to muster the courage to shout at a few people and organise myself a lift back to the hotel, but that would only happen after Jimi Hendrix had been on. The concert was running later and later, and by the time he did appear it was well into the early hours, and he then set about playing a long, long set to an audience all of whom bar one seemed ecstatic. I was vaguely aware that he was up there on stage being brilliant. I can still remember the whining soaring adrenalin-boosting sound of his guitar, but, hardly able to keep my eyes open, I couldn't wait for him to finish so I could go.

Next morning I went home as soon as I was able, and am probably the only living person who attended one of the historic Isle of Wight Festivals, saw both The Doors and Hendrix perform, had access all areas, and came home convinced that it had been one of the most miserable weekends of my life. Let's put it this way – it was another thirty years before I ever went near another festival in the UK, and that was to see my own son Chris perform.

Eighteen days later, Jimi Hendrix was dead. And I didn't see the Kid again for a few years by which time he was happily married with a dog and a baby, living near Sherwood Forest and working for Radio Trent.

But a few months later I did find out a bit more about what had gone wrong that weekend between the Kid and me. I had to interview Tony Prince on the phone and in the middle of the conversation he suddenly said, 'Why did you blow Kid out that weekend at the Isle of Wight?'

Taken aback, I said, 'What do you mean – I didn't blow him out! He blew me out! He was with Anne Challis!'

'Oh Judy you are so silly. Why do you think I wrote that note for him to give you? He couldn't wait to see you. But he is shy. I thought you would read the note and all would be great.'

'Well he was with her all the time and he didn't even talk to me. She was in his bedroom.'

'Judy, he didn't fancy her. He wasn't sleeping with her. He didn't want her in his bedroom, she just followed him around the place. It was you he wanted. When you read the note and you didn't do anything, he thought you didn't want him any more ... he was gutted ...'

Many, many years later I did meet up with Kid again – we both felt we had 'unfinished business' to talk through. At that meeting, he told me that in fact Anne was gay. And when he said that, I remembered, so clearly, the time she turned up unannounced in my office at *Fab*, bearing a packet of cigarettes for me. At the time I couldn't understand why she'd done it. But perhaps, just perhaps, it was me she had her eye on, not Kid at all.

Some things just aren't meant to be. We both ended up happily married to other people, but do you ever greedily feel that just one single passage through life somehow isn't enough?

Around the time of the mix-up with Kid that kept us apart, I had had other things on my mind as well and was still trying to get over one.

I realised I was pregnant just one week after I got back from that first Radio Luxembourg trip in late April 1970. When I had been out there, I began to realise something wasn't quite right with my body. I had been sitting with Kid in his room, on his bed, wearing my best miniskirt and tight top, and we had been having a discussion about size and shape.

'I hate my body' I said. 'I am too thin.' And he said, 'No, you're not – you're not thin at all.' I looked down at myself and realised that he was right, I wasn't really thin any more. And, more pertinent – I seemed to be developing a fat stomach. I shut up about my size, and back in my hotel room stripped off, turned sideways and looked at myself in the mirror. My belly was most definitely sticking out. And it was hard, firm. I began to have a nasty feeling that something was far from right.

Back at home, I returned to work and developed a strong and urgent craving for oranges, day and night. I was in the

Ladies at Fleetway three days after I got home, sitting on the loo, wondering if I'd ever have a period again (they'd never been that regular), craving an orange, gazing at my fat belly, when I noticed a dark line going from my navel downwards.

And then I knew with a certain horror that I was pregnant. And there could only be one father. A man who had been in my life, in quite a casual way, for the past few months. A man who, again, was married, had three children of his own, one of whom was only just born – and who was my boss.

I couldn't have got it much more wrong.

I had been warned off him several times by Betty Hale – and he himself later told me, laughing wildly at the joke, that she had confronted him when he arrived as our publishing boss, saying, 'Now, don't you go anywhere near my girls!' He had a reputation as a ladies' man, and very deserved it was.

Being the kind of person who hates being told I can't do something, as soon as Betty warned me to stay away from him as he was a) married and b) a womaniser – I couldn't resist. Of course I couldn't. He often drank in the Hoop and Grapes, and so did I. He was personable, charming, slim, blonde and with a great smile. I was young, with long hair and long legs.

So the inevitable happened – eventually we got together. At the time, I found out later, he was just finishing a relationship with another girl who had worked for him, who also had a guy of her own. These were the dying days of the Swinging era, the pill was easy to get (not that I was on it), and that is what one did. The world of publishing was very incestuous and it seemed that at one time or another, everybody 'screwed' (the word of the day for partaking in sexual intercourse) everybody else. Compared with most of them, I was a true innocent.

He was still living with his family and I am sure thought of me as nothing more than a passing amusement – we certainly had little more than a 'drink in the pub occasionally followed by a taxi home to my bedsit, sex' kind of relationship. Apart from anything else, I was terrified that Betty would find out and find a reason to sack me.

I was chatting with Georgina in the office one day a few months earlier after the first time I had slept with The Boss, and she offered me three months' supply of the pill, which she had got for herself and then decided not to take. Gratefully I took them from her and began them.

As it turned out, it was already too late and I must have been pregnant after the first time we slept together towards the end of December 1969.

After that day in the loo, I went to my GP near Avonmore Road who within a few days confirmed my pregnancy. He arranged for me to see a consultant in Wimpole Street and I was given a price, £80 (over £900 in today's money), for an abortion. The next time I saw The Boss, I told him I was pregnant, said I wanted an abortion and could he pay me something towards the cost please?

In the end he paid half, and my sister, who was one of the few people I had told, lent me the other half. For some reason, which escapes me now, I also told Betty, who to my surprise was brilliant, and Heather Kirby, our fashion editor, who was a complete brick throughout it all and even picked me up from the hospital afterwards.

That abortion is another thing, like the Bertie Green episode, that I totally erased from my mind after it happened. There was little to consider re pros and cons.

I was four and a half months pregnant but it never really entered my head to keep the baby. The father was married and my boss, I was 20, I saw no way to raise a baby on my income – or, indeed, to continue with my job if I had a baby, I lived in a no-babies-allowed house, and could not see myself as a mother at all. My mother, who around this time was living with and looking after my gran, and who had fairly poor health, was in no position to help me look after a baby either.

What kept me going throughout was the thought of the Kid and when I might see him again. It was a good job I didn't know how the Isle of Wight would turn out.

But from time to time, even now all these years later, although I can't/don't want to remember which hospital it was, or the exact date of the abortion, or anything much else about that time – I do remember giving birth to the foetus. I was too far gone for an ordinary scraping and so had had a birth-inducing injection in my belly. After several hours of fairly serious agony, the nurse brought a stainless steel tray and squatted me over it on the bed. A few minutes later, I pushed the foetus out. I remember looking down at it, all pink and curled and about the size of a kitten, and wondering what sex it was, before the nurse came and took it away.

A couple of weeks later, Betty and Heather decided to 'give' me another press trip abroad, to help me, I am sure, 'get over' what had happened in the past couple of months.

This time the visit was to a Swedish music festival, where I was to interview ordinary Swedish teenagers about their lives, their make-up routines and whatever.

The plan was to get the plane out of Heathrow with our photographer Roger Brown, all the music press people and some of the English stars who were appearing at the festival. We'd go straight to the festival, stay the night, then fly back the next day.

That was my first experience of P.J. Proby, the singer who had made his reputation, mainly, by splitting his pants on stage but whom I had always admired as I thought he had a great voice.

P.J. was due to appear at the concert and was on the plane, getting fairly tanked up on the free booze. By the time we were nearing Arlanda airport, Stockholm, Proby was staggering about the aisles, singing and trying to tell us all jokes and stories. And the air hostesses were trying to get him to sit down. He pulled one of them down onto his lap where she kept him busy and pinned down while we landed, thus saving us from having to go around again and perhaps circle for an hour or two. P.J. continued to play to the crowds at the airport as we waited for baggage and it is hard to believe that he managed to perform only a few hours later, but perform (on stage, that is) he did, and quite well, too.

We were driven through the Swedish countryside for mile upon mile – me staring out of the coach window and wondering how any country could be so beautiful but so bland and boring and sterile all at the same time. In other words, I didn't like it much.

By the time Roger and I reached the festival, having also had our share of alcohol, I wanted nothing more than to go to sleep but had to knuckle down and find lots of teenybopper Swedes to interview and photograph. Every time we found a really pretty one, she didn't speak enough English so it took a long time, and I seem to remember making most of these interviews up when I got home in the hope that the Swedish girls definitely wouldn't be finding copies of *Fab* or translating their 'quotes'.

Heading the bill at the festival were a band of hairy Americans called, I am pretty sure, Blood, Sweat & Tears – proper rock merchants whose set I found distinctly underwhelming and which also gave me a nasty headache. That said, they were one of the top bands of the day. I just had little taste, that's what it was.

After a couple of hours sleep it was back to the airport and the UK. One thing I will say – Jim Proby was a lot quieter on the way home. But after we said goodbye at Heathrow and he went off, smiling his nice crinkly smile, I kind of missed him for a while. He was a good bloke. Next time I saw him some years later, he was Elvis.

Whether or not the visit to Sweden was the tonic I needed after the events of May I am not sure – on balance, probably not. I was knackered for a week after.

Over the next year I saw little of The Boss ... there is nothing quite like an abortion to put a tarnish on a budding romance. On my 21st birthday, on 6 August 1970, I went out to dinner at an Italian restaurant down the Fulham Road with Georgina and her boyfriend Roy. If she hadn't taken me out, I would have been on my own. So much for my fabulous life.

A few weeks later, The Boss did buy me a small dried flower ornament – which I still have today – as a belated present, at which point I realised that the affair hadn't been extinguished along with the life, just put on ice for a while.

Gradually, after a few months of emotional turmoil, by the end of 1970 I began to find things about life to enjoy once again. My diary says that I met Robin Gibb, Simon Dee, Matt Monro, Rod Steiger, Dionne Warwick and Martin Jarvis that year – but there were many more. I remember travelling down to Jenny Agutter's home in a peaceful spot outside London – at 17, she was a huge star because of *The Railway Children* but was about as shy and quiet as I had been at her age.

The diaries are slightly frustrating to look through now because I only kept them in a very offhand, perfunctory irregular way – sometimes you'll find a page saying, 'Rod Steiger, 11.30, Dionne Warwick, 2.00, driving lesson 3.00, dentist, 4.00.' or 'Monday, David Essex, Tuesday, The Osmonds, Wednesday, Paul McCartney, Thursday, buy egg poacher'. I think I was too busy living and doing to keep a diary properly. In September I booked a holiday to Holland with my mother – the only proper holiday she and I ever had together alone, and the first time she had been abroad since a school visit to Paris when she was very young. Why we chose Holland I am not sure, unless it was that Mother wanted to try to find her long-lost relatives – her grandfather had come to England from Amsterdam as a child.

We caught a ferry to Ostend, then boarded a tour coach which took us through Belgium and Holland, finally arriving at the town of Valkenburg in the only hilly part of the country, in the south-east near the German border.

We had a great week, going down the Rhine, wine tasting, sightseeing and generally enjoying ourselves, and in any boring moments I could regale Mother with many of my show business tales. She had always had a great interest in the world of showbiz and some of the glamour of my job rubbed off on her – she loved it when she saw my picture or byline here and there, and when I had gone to the premiere of *The Magic Christian*, my mother was there in the crowd to watch me, loving every second of it – and loving the tales later of how I had shaken hands with Peter Sellers and Ringo Starr and seen Princess Margaret and Lord Snowdon this far away, so close I could see the violet of her eyes and the hair in his ears.

She quite often came up to Avonmore Road to stay for a few days and, if she was well enough, we always got up to mischief. Back in Buckingham, Mother didn't get out a lot – she was no longer friends with Mrs Hill, whose lobotomy had turned out not to be as successful as had been hoped; her sadistic tendencies had begun to return and Mother had decided it was best to give her a wide berth. Not before time, is what I thought.

By the time we returned from our autumn holiday, I was more or less back on track. Most evenings I would go out with Julie or occasionally Georgina, Nigel or one or other of the guys I knew from the music press. Gordon Coxhill was still around and I was friendly with Roy Carr, another journalist on the *NME*, who had an encyclopaedic knowledge of music and a music collection to match – once Julie and I visited his small flat in the city and it was like a cave chock full, ceiling to floor, with vinyl. He lived for music and should have been another John Peel.

He may have fancied his chances with me a bit but he never did anything about it. He wasn't one of the world's greatest lookers – he had a ZZ Topp kind of beard and a rather hunched posture, always wore a black leather jacket and just didn't have a lot of sex appeal but he was a truly lovely man. Roy, I think, realised that I was in a marginal depression that autumn and took charge to ensure that I wasn't hanging around Avonmore Road on my own too much.

One day in October we drove down to the Orchid Ballroom, Purley after work to see The Who. The place was small and considering The Who were by now very big, having released *Tommy* and broken the USA, it was really too small a venue for them to gig. But they liked doing small places in between the stadiums, so there we were in this ballroom surrounded by crazed Who fans pushing and shoving and for reasons I will never understand, the stage had been built way too high, so that wherever you were in the room, you had to crane your head backwards as far as you could to get a look at the band.

They played to an ecstatic crowd for probably nearly two hours – certainly by the time the set ended I had a hugely bad pain in the neck, a monstrous headache and was slightly worried because my escort appeared to have vanished in the crowd.

Roy knew everybody in the music business and quite a few media people had been invited down to Purley. But he did return to find me, squashed and wishing I'd not had high heels on, at the end of the gig.

It was only a few weeks later that I got the chance to see The Who again – Julie had been invited to their gig at the Hammersmith Palais which, I believe, was the last night of their little autumn tour. We arranged to meet there as I had a film screening to attend beforehand.

I arrived at the Palais and pressed through the crowds – I could see this was going to be a wild night even by Who standards – backstage to find no sign of Julie, but the members of The Who trying to get themselves dressed and ready for the gig. A few familiar faces were there from the music papers but I didn't know them that well so settled into a corner to wait for Julie. No show, so I crossed the room to help myself to some drink. When I got back there was Keith Moon, rifling through the handbag that I'd left on a table.

'Er, Keith – hi! That's my bag.'

The Moon turned round, his face in that expression you've seen in photos a hundred times, naughty, cheeky little boy. 'Oh sorry, love, sorry, I was just looking for this ...'

And he held up my best Biba lipstick. 'You don't mind do you?'

Well I wasn't going to say no. 'Well of course go ahead ... but I'm not sure it's the right shade for you ...'.

He laughed and retreated with his prize to his corner of the room and I watched fascinated to see what he was going to do with my lipstick. He removed his T-shirt and proceeded to draw an intricate pattern with it on his fairly hairless chest, finishing by drawing concentric circles round each nipple. Then he put his T-shirt back on and sauntered over to me again. 'Thanks!'

And he handed me back my lipstick – or I should say, the empty container as he'd used every bit of it on his body.

He was so sweet though that you couldn't be cross with him.

After the support act had finished and Julie had turned up, we made our way out front where a sea of bodies was pressing into the stage. The Who came out, Keith looking demure in his white T-shirt, and proceeded to do a fantastic end-of-tour set.

The mob got wilder and wilder and I managed to retreat to the back of the room where there was space to breathe. Shortly before the end of the set, off came Keith's T-shirt and I stood there looking at this crazy little guy, drumming wildly and wearing my lipstick on his chest.

You know what emotion I felt? I felt proud he was wearing my lipstick and proud to be part of this scene. Part of me realised that this time was something special, that The Who would be recognised as one of the greatest rock bands of the twentieth century. But by far the biggest of my emotions was sorrow and guilt – because the lipstick was too muted a colour to be seen properly under the lights. Poor Keith! If only I had bought the bright red Chanel, not the dusky Biba! That's what I thought.

The set ended with Pete smashing up his guitar. The Who had become famous for the amount of equipment that was wrecked on stage, but you didn't always get to see this; it hadn't happened at Purley. So if a guitar got smashed you felt, kind of privileged to witness it. As the boys left the stage, the audience carried on rioting and fighting, and I slipped out and walked the few minutes home to my room, the sounds of the crowd and 'My Generation' and 'I Can't Explain' ringing in my head as I strode through the dimly lit, deserted back streets of West Kensington at the end of another 'ordinary' day.

A day when I saw Pete Townshend break his guitar. And Keith Moon stole my lipstick.

I kept that lipstick container for some while as a unique souvenir of Moonie and an incredible evening.

six

Just Call
My Name

1971

Shillings and pence have gone – it's 'p' now when you want to buy a single. Mick Jagger's married Bianca. God, the charts and TV schedules are full of rubbish – plenty of naff stuff around this year. 'Grandad' by Clive Dunn; 'Chirpy Chirpy Cheep Cheep' from Middle of the Road, and Benny Hill with 'Ernie'; *The Cilla Black Show*, *It's a Knockout* and *Dixon of Dock Green*, winding down to a merciful death. We're saved only by T.Rex and Slade.

1970 had certainly helped me achieve my main ambition – less beauty and film, more music. But I was still doing a mix of all three – and, later in the year, I would be very glad that I was still covering movies.

By early 1971 it seemed that the little office in Old Fleetway inhabited by Georgina and I had been visited by thousands of pop promotors and PRs. But one I remember better than most. He appeared at the door when, for once, I was busy trying to work. Even now I can picture his boyish, enthusiastic face, his short hair, his suit and tie and his dark overcoat. He looked nothing like most of the people in the music business looked at that time, i.e. – he looked straight, very straight, in the old-fashioned sense of conservative.

This guy, I'd guess, was trying to look older than he was, which, I imagine, was about the same age as me, but it just wasn't creating the right impression. Clutching a set of 45s and a sheaf of photos, he grinned widely and announced, in an American accent, he'd come to talk about The Osmonds.

'THE OSMONDS!?!?' shrieked Georgina.

'You mean THE OSMOND BROTHERS?!' I shouted. 'That bunch of cheesy American kids who used to sing barbershop songs on The Andy Williams Show back when I was still living at home and my dad and I used to watch the show on our old black and white TV at Weston on the Green?' I asked. '*Those* Osmonds?!'

Yes, it was true – he'd really come on behalf of the Osmond brothers. Georgina and I both sat there and laughed at him.

This, you remember, was around the time that the Rolling Stones were charting with the *Sticky Fingers* album, T.Rex were high in the singles charts with *Hot Love* and Rod Stewart and his Faces were cavorting around the stage in loon pants and tight flowery shirts.

'The Osmond Brothers – what do you think they're going to do here then?' we enquired.

'Well I have to tell you guys they're really big in the States now. They're not called the Osmonds Brothers any more, just The Osmonds. They've changed their image a lot, they sing real rock, they play instruments, they're groovy now. Really, honestly, trust me!'

With that he shoved a single under my nose and we played it. He was quite determined not to go away until we had. 'One Bad Apple'.

'Oh no – it sounds just like The Jackson Five, but not as good! They're never going to get anywhere. And aren't they Mormons?'

We looked at the photo – and there were five boys all with huge sets of gleaming teeth and short dark hair cut into pudding basins *a la* early Beatles but not quite as cool, a couple of them with tubby faces too. Not rock gods in the making even if you didn't know they were the Osmond brothers.

Anyway the American guy wouldn't have his faith in these boys dampened and away he went promising us that the boys were going to be huge in the UK.

We were giggling about that all day, on and off.

But, of course, The Osmonds had the last laugh because indeed they did become huge in the UK as well as in many other parts of the world. It took a while – 'One Bad Apple' didn't go down that well in the UK, reaching only number 44, and their follow up later in 1971, 'Down by the Lazy River', did only marginally better. However, by 1972 they were massive … and they became a huge part of my working life for several years.

But Bill, the American, clean-cut guy, he also had the last laugh in a much more personal way. His flair for publicity and his determination were, I believe, one of the major reasons that The Osmonds did finally find their place in the UK. He worked tremendously hard for them and I ended up with great respect for him, his dedication to the cause and his ability to get people to do what he wanted them to do.

A few years down the line he and the boys parted company and I almost forgot all about him for decades. Then I switched on ITV thirty-five years later in 2006 and saw a face I couldn't help but recognise, one of the judges on a popular talent show of that year, *Soapstar Superstar*.

Bill had morphed into 'Billy' Sammeth, apparently, while I wasn't looking, having built up one of the biggest star management outfits in the USA with Cher and numerous other stars in his stable.

Turned out okay for him, then. And very pleased I am too. Moral: never underestimate young men in suits.

A little later in the year I headed down to Sussex to a rather beautiful old house lost in the middle of nowhere, to spend a Sunday with Adam Faith, his wife Jackie – the girl he had 'stolen' from Cliff Richard, so the story went, some years before – and their newborn baby, Katya.

Adam had, for many years in the early '60s, been one of the UK's top pop stars along with Billy Fury and Cliff Richard, but by this time he had just become famous on British TV as an actor in a series called *Budgie*.

I didn't tell him that seven or so years previously I had paid to watch him on stage at the New Theatre, Oxford. He hadn't been much of a singer, and he was tiny (about 5ft 4 or 5in), but he had a beautiful face.

They were superb hosts and proudly showed me all around the property, which they'd bought and done up from scratch. I found out later that this was a hobby as well as another way of making money, and that they never stayed anywhere for too long – buy it, do it up, sell it. Adam was a canny guy and I wasn't surprised when in later years he became a financial guru.

He was also becoming a shrewd music manager and the following year he would discover his biggest act – Leo Sayer; derided at the time for his hair, his voice and his songs but in 2006, a comeback kid with a remixed number one. Who would have thought?

Another huge TV star in the same year was Peter Wyngarde, star of mega TV series *Department S*. I popped down to his huge apartment in Battersea one day to do an interview. While he looked the part – the sex symbol with his velvet jackets, cravats and ludicrous moustache, who would get through several woman every week as Jason King – he was strangely nervy and on edge all the time I was there. Perhaps he had a wardrobe full of young men and was frightened they'd escape and he would be outed.

Homosexuality had only been legalised in the UK in 1967 and very many of the gay actors were still running scared.

Later in the year, *Fab 208* magazine moved from the Fleetway offices up to 32 Southampton Street in Covent Garden. I moved into an office of my own, with an interconnecting door to Georgina's office. Although I had loved my years 'on' Fleet Street, the Farringdon Road area was run down to say the least, while the area off the Strand was much more central and near more pubs and shops. The old Covent Garden fruit and veg market was still in place and I'd occasionally pop round the corner from the office for lunch (usually liquid) at Rules in Maiden Lane. The Boss, whom I was seeing on a regular basis by this time, had left Fleetway (which was to become IPC Magazines) and was working as a PR for Rules, and seemed to have virtually free run of the drink and food in the place.

Meanwhile the press receptions for a never-ending stream of singers, bands, musicians, actors and would-be famous people continued unabated and one had to exercise a small amount of self-discipline and discerning choice in order not to spend most of each working day out of the office, getting no writing done.

One I chose to go to, wearing my crushed brown velvet hotpants and brown patent platform shoes, was a thrash for Ike and Tina Turner – now I wonder why that word came out just then? Anyway, at the time none of us in the music business was aware, as far as I know, that Ike and Tina's marriage and professional partnership was under a great deal of strain and that Ike had, on occasion, a somewhat physical way of dealing with the problems.

So off I went to this particular shindig, being quite a fan of some of their music, in particular 'River Deep Mountain High' which never failed to make me feel just fantastic whenever I heard it on the radio or in a disco. I believe they were doing a tour of Europe at the time and had one or two live gigs in London. Anyway the press reception was buzzing, the Turners were working the room (a sure sign that they needed us more than we needed them – the big stars would sit in a large chair in a corner and their PRs would 'allow' the chosen few to go and see them, and the super-mega-stars might even just arrive in the room towards the end of the 'do', entourage all around, wave a hand, pose for a couple of photos and then depart) and after half an hour or so they introduced themselves and began chatting to me. Ike seemed distracted for some reason but I found Tina easy to talk to and after a few minutes her voice, which was quite in your face talking as well as singing, quietened and she leant towards me.

'Do you want a job?' she stage whispered.

Now this quite took me back; it wasn't really what I was expecting her to come out with. I would have been less surprised by, say, 'Fancy a shag with Ike in our hotel tonight?' or, 'Can I borrow your comb?'

'Err…'. I smiled tentatively, trying to work out what the right response was. I didn't think I wanted a job, I already had one I was enjoying no end – but it isn't every day of the week that a leading international singing star sidles up to you and says that.

'What kind of job?' I said eventually.

'Well, working for me and Ike! We're looking for a new PA and we want you.'

Well talk about making your mind up on minimal information. I should have asked Tina what it was about me that so took them so suddenly. Desperation, most likely. After all, my reputation for shorthand hadn't exactly gone before me, well not in a good way, anyhow. But she'd thrown me off balance and all I managed to say was a pathetic:

'Can I let you know later?' Nothing about 'What does the job entail? What's the pay? When would I start? What are the freebies? What are the hours?'

At this point she must have realised that I was an idiot and not PA material in any way. But next minute she was scribbling out their contact details on some paper and, I assumed, making sure the phone number was false; it's only what I would have done myself, had I been her.

'Here – can you call me by tomorrow?' and she was off, with her tight short skirt and her huge hair and her famous walk, to the other side of the room. I thought she was fabulous fun.

Well I went back to work, thought about it some – it could be an incredible experience, I figured – went home, thought about it some more, and woke up in the night, realising with certainty that there was no way I could chuck in my job and go and work for two people I didn't know, in the States, no matter what the job entailed or how much the pay was. I didn't feel I'd exhausted all the possibilities of the job I was already doing … not by miles.

So I rang up the number as promised, quite shocked to find it really did put me through to Tina Turner, and apologised and said no.

Looking back, I guess whoever had been their PA immediately before had just walked, and left them in the lurch – hence Ike's distracted air and Tina's homing in on me; it really was desperation, I reckon. In later years the very bad state of their marriage and working relationship was revealed in a movie – at the time of the job offer, it would have been meltdown – and I have never felt so glad about my inbuilt sense of caution that sometimes, but not always, overcame the wilder ideas and opportunities that came my way every now and then.

In April I was contacted by the press officer for the film company making a movie called *Catlow* which was to star Yul Brynner and a long list of mostly B-list actors including Richard Crenna, Dahlia Lavi and Alan Ladd's son David. Also making his first movie since leaving Star Trek was Leonard Nimoy – Mr pointy-eared Spock himself.

They would be filming in Almeria, Spain, in May and I was invited to go over there, all expenses paid, with photographer, to watch filming and meet the cast, in return for publishing a feature on Brynner. Well, it sounded like quite a good freebie. Although I'd never really liked Yul Brynner, I fancied a few days of sun and Sangria and anyway the Ed wanted me to go.

The Saturday before we flew from Heathrow to Almeria I went shopping down Kensington High Street – easy walking distance from the bedsit – to buy some lightweight items. At the time, the height of fashion was a loose smock top with matching hotpants, so I bought myself a set, a couple of floppy hats from Barkers and some sun cream.

And on Thursday 20 May, the photographer – who's name was, I believe, Roger Morton – and I arrived in Almeria to be met at the airport by the film's PR man, Brian, a slightly tubby guy in suit and tie – the swinging '60s and '70s had completely passed him by and no matter how hot it got or how many drinks he had I never saw him less than immaculate in his city outfits.

I secretly felt rather full of myself, sole journalist, being met with a posh car to go to a film set to visit the great Yul Brynner, being put up in Almeria's finest hotel (whatever that was, can't remember) with a big bowl of fruit and flowers waiting for me in the room – now this was the life! I hadn't travelled much for *Fab* and what travelling I had done had more in common with slumming it than with living it up, that's for sure. But this was a bit swish, if there was such a thing as swish in southern Spain in the early '70s.

The next day we were escorted by Brian to the indoor set to watch Brynner do a scene. I remember his wife, a tall, slim blonde woman, sitting there knitting furiously. And I remember getting more and more agitated as Brynner worked through his scene, knowing that when he finished I was expected to talk to him.

It was a return of my feelings of inferiority that had plagued me backstage at the Isle of Wight – he looked so fierce, he never smiled. I just stood there getting smaller and smaller, all sensible thoughts and questions slipping and dripping from my mind. And I didn't even have a hangover.

But I couldn't get out of it. He came over, bald at the front but with a plaited ponytail down his back, shortish, but tough, tough, tough eyes looking through you. I had vaguely hoped that once his scene was finished he would morph into a laughy, jokey, smiley kind of guy who couldn't wait to put a silly little English fan mag journalist at her ease – but no. It was as bad as I had thought it would be. I would ask a question, he would give a one word reply. I would ask another question, same. Same, same.

After a few minutes I turned to his wife and began to ask her questions instead, and got much more out of her; she was charming. But Brynner – when I got home and told my mother what I thought of him, she was incredulous. He'd been a long-time idol of hers – and I hadn't even bothered to get her his autograph.

But the trip began to look up in a big way when I was introduced to Mr Spock. I'd always had a quiet fascination for him in his TV role but had never thought of him as the sort of man I could fancy; a caesar haircut and big pointy ears had never been my things. I hadn't come on this press trip even to see him, really, so I hadn't boned up on him at all and knew next to nothing about him and his life.

But it took me about two minutes flat having been introduced to Nimoy to realise that he was completely stunning. WOW. It was the first time I grasped that sex appeal often has little to do with classic good looks or a head of blonde hair or broad shoulders.

Leonard Nimoy was nearly twenty years older than me. He had smallish eyes, a wide mouth, a long nose, a thin frame, a beard (oh how I never liked beards!), glasses, dark thinning hair and nondescript clothes .... and he was sex on legs, even more so that Jim Dale, my first interview that seemed so long ago now.

Was it the deep honey voice, was it that he had the knack of making you feel you were stunningly beautiful and fabulously interesting? Was it the blue eyes, which sparkled full of mischief even when he was being serious? The warm, dry handshake that did it, or the truly gorgeous smile that came out of nowhere?

Whatever – I was lovestruck, and, even better, I could talk to him, and even better still, I liked him. And he seemed to like me.

We went back to his apartment – a dark, dark place because all the shutters had been closed to keep out the heat. We drank sangria, talked and laughed a lot and arranged to meet up the next morning when he would take me for a walk up into the hills to see Almeria's fort.

Every evening most of the cast and crew – with the exception of Brynner and Nimoy – would meet up in the restaurant of the hotel where we were staying, for a meal, lots of wine, and plenty of chat and laughter.

Over the dinner table that first night I found out that Leonard Nimoy was not only married, but that his wife was here with him. I felt devastated enough to have trouble eating anything. Of course, I had been stupid to think he liked me. Of course, he was just acting, just being pleasant so that I would write nice things about him. Of course.

Next day, knowing I still had to keep our 'date' I made sure that Roger came along too. Nimoy came to collect me – did I detect a crestfallen look when he saw someone else with me? I think so – and off we set up the hills of the old town to the ancient fort, me trying hard to be cool and professional and avoid any kind of flirting or the easiness we'd had between us the day before.

Having done little in the way of exercise except drinking and dancing for several years, I was pretty unfit and after a hundred or so steep narrow steps, was puffing and panting in a far from sexy fashion. Nimoy saved the day by grabbing my hand to help me along, and continued to hold it firmly and warmly from that moment right to the end of the walk.

How well I remember trying hard to keep aloof but feeling quite blissfully happy about this, feeling some kind of electric current running between the two of us, forgetting all about Roger, and about Nimoy's wife. She wasn't here. I couldn't pretend to be cold towards him any more, I just couldn't do it. We sat around the fort walls for a while, we talked, we laughed, we just sat. Roger, quite obviously, felt like a spare part and spent most of his time wandering around well out of our way.

As we sat, Nimoy gave me what was probably the most sensual, fabulous and tender, real, lingering and unforgettable kiss I had ever had.

Later, I somehow managed to pluck up the nerve to ask Nimoy about his wife: 'Oh, she's gone to Madrid shopping,' he said. That was all he ever said about her.

Eventually we headed back down the hill and he had to go to get ready for some night filming. The next time I saw him he was on set. I watched filming of a street scene with Crenna and Dahlia Lavi on horseback during which Leonard and I took breaks at the refreshment van together once or twice – but were never alone again.

The next day Roger and I were booked on a flight home and Leonard had made me promise to come and say goodbye before we left. Back at his apartment, he came outside. His wife may have been inside, but I never met her. Nimoy gave me a long but chaste kiss on the lips and a long and warm hug.

'Can't you stay a bit longer?' he said. 'Do you really have to go?'

I said I did.

'Stay in touch,' he said. 'Ask Brian. Come back over, we're here for several more weeks …'

I forced myself simply to smile but not answer.

I didn't want to leave the man, and as I forced myself to put one leg in front of the other to get in the car waiting to take us to the airport, it felt like there was a length of extra strong elastic holding us both together, holding me back, making each step feel more difficult than the last. I forced myself to wave and smile at him as we went, as if I didn't care. I forced myself on to the plane and sat crying most of the way home. Roger did his best to cheer me up.

'You really liked each other, didn't you?' he said.

'Was it that obvious?'

'Yes of course it was …'

'Do you think he liked me, really?'

'Yes, he liked you really. Why don't you call him when you get home?'

The fact is, if Nimoy hadn't been married, I would have done anything in my power to spend more time with him, to get to know him. I would have missed the flight and stayed there with him. But he was married, and there didn't seem any point. He wouldn't have brought her with him if they weren't a real proper item, I reasoned. I must have misread the signals, I must have got it all wrong. The fact that I had been dating a married man, The Boss, on and off for some time didn't cross my mind.

Back at home, I had the photos Roger had taken, I had my canvas *Catlow* bag, and that was it. However, I couldn't stop thinking about him. Okay – I had been taken in by men before, and since. But I am sure that guy was truly interested in me, I am sure there were real feelings between us and if I hadn't been a journalist I think he would have done something more about it.

When the movie came out at the end of that year I had more or less got over Mr Spock because you have to – but how really, really, annoyed I was when I found out in the press that not all that long afterwards, Mr and Mrs Nimoy split up.

Eventually, Nimoy found himself a younger woman. She looked a bit like me. Well, that's what I like to think.

That year The Boss and I were still seeing each other from time to time, though I am pretty sure he was having flings with various women and I was just one of them.

Other than that the rest of my year, romance-wise, was pretty dead.

I still did the occasional beauty piece and would go to very occasional cosmetics functions if I hadn't anything better to do – one of which was a press party for Goya, the large firm which had been one of the best-known names in UK cosmetics and perfume for some time and which was worth a fortune.

There I was introduced to Tim Collins, the son of the owners of Goya. Tim took a real shine to me and by the end of the party had asked me out for a dinner date.

He was a charming young man, rather tubby, very clean cut, pleasant to look at, but sadly he most definitely wasn't another Nimoy – he definitely wasn't for me. Even so – I went on the date. I think I hoped he would somehow bring out his hidden wow factor, a previously disguised cache of sex appeal, and bowl me over after all. So we went to dinner, him picking me up at Avonmore Road in his Roller (bet that was the first and last time he ever went to a tacky bedsit to collect a girl and I bet it was the only time he had a Polish landlady standing on the door exclaiming at the car and waving us off!).

We had a pleasant date at a posh Mayfair restaurant and Tim asked to see me again – but I couldn't face it. I so wanted to be the kind of girl who could see a rich guy at a thousand paces one day, get him proposing to her the next, and marry him shortly afterwards, henceforth to live in extremely comfortable, lazy, marital bliss with homes all over the world before getting a mega payout on divorce day – but I couldn't do it. If I didn't fancy someone, all the money in the world couldn't get me enthused.

I went to one other interesting film set but this time it was only at Twickenham studios – *The Straw Dogs* was filming, with Dustin Hoffman, Susan George, and a few smaller time actors including Colin Welland who later became very well known in the UK as a playwright. Dustin Hoffman was another of those guys who could wow you with his sex appeal even though he was very short and not classically attractive. But he wasn't a patch on Spock.

The highlight of my October was meeting another of the bands who had helped me through my early teenage years – The Everly Brothers, who were about to make a comeback with RCA after several years in the wilderness overshadowed by the new wave rock bands. They had a press reception in town and I had a few words with both of them, particularly my old favourite, Phil. But it wasn't my first meeting with them – not that I was going to remind them of the first.

It's 1965. I'm 16 at last. I'm sitting at the tiny fold-down table in the caravan at Botley where I live with my mother and the cat. We moved here a few months ago when Mum and Dad split up for the second time; he went to live in a bedsit in Cowley and we came here to this small fixed van estate; it was all we could afford. I'm studying for my A levels at Oxford Technical College. I'm supposed to be working on economic history but in fact have more than half an ear on the radio ... the pirate station Radio London, the Dave Cash show.

I hear he's announcing a competition. '… I'm going to play the start of an old hit and if you can guess the song and send your answer in on a postcard, you could win two tickets to a fab pop show in London …'. So I'm all ears. Within one second I identify the song as 'Crying in the Rain', the famous Everly Brothers song from 1961. 'I'll never let you see, just how my broken heart is hearting me …'

So it's away with the books, out with a postcard, con Mum for a stamp and off it's posted. And I win. A couple of weeks later I'm heading to London with my friend Cookie. We get there on the coach then somehow I negotiate us to East Ham tube station and to the Granada Theatre. And then we're allowed on stage to meet The Everly Brothers, and an hour or two later at last I'm sitting there watching my heroes from way back, perform all their hits. Including 'Cathy's Clown' and 'Crying in the Rain'. It's magic. Magic. How lucky I am. I just don't want to go home. I want to stay here forever and listen to pop music.

Press reception and new recording contract or not, I was disturbed by how anxious The Everlys seemed, twitchy and strained. I came away with the impression they really didn't want to be doing this.

A year or two later I was to find out that by the time of that reception, Don and Phil were both having personal problems and arguing all the time. In the summer of 1973 Phil smashed his guitar to pieces on stage, walked out, and they didn't perform together again for many years. But no other duo in pop has ever touched them for the true pop quality of their songs and their fabulous voices and pretty faces.

On 19 November I met for the first time two bands who were to become perhaps the biggest UK pop bands of the '70s – in the morning, the Bay City Rollers, a band from Edinburgh who had been struggling to get a foot on the pop ladder for a couple of years and were being pushed hard by manager Tam Paton.

While I found the boys – brothers Alan and Derek Longmuir, Woody, Les and Eric – nice enough lads, their single 'Keep on Dancing' was barely average and it was, in my mind, similar to how I felt about The Osmonds – they just weren't going to get anywhere, no matter how loud their managers shouted that they were.

Well, I was right, for a while at least. 'Keep on Dancing' spent seven weeks slowly creeping up the charts to finally reach a high of number 9, from whence it slowly disappeared as did the Bay City Rollers, more or less, for another three years or more. At which point they became, more or less, as big as The Beatles for a while. And I was proved wrong again.

Later that day I headed to John Halsall's office to meet a new (well, new in terms of the charts) band from Wolverhampton, Slade. John Halsall had, for a time, dated Julie Webb, we all knew each other very well and he was building up a good business for himself in promotion and PR. Slade, under the guidance of Chas Chandler (who was one of the most respected names in the music business, having made stars in the UK both of The Animals and Jimi Hendrix) had at last come out of the wilderness of several years of touring the provinces as a quasi-skinhead band. They'd grown their hair, and were now at number 1 in the charts with 'Coz I Luv You'.

Noddy, Jim, Dave and Don were four great guys whom I immediately liked as they were quick-witted, warm people who didn't take themselves too seriously and were completely down to earth. That song stayed in the top 10 for seven weeks and was the start of a huge career for them. Even I could see the potential in this batty band. They seemed to be saying: Look … the '60s are history. This is the '70s. This is our time. And don't you forget it …

Slade soon became good mates and I usually saw them up at the BBC TV Centre in Wood Lane, where they always seemed to be doing *Top of the Pops*. This was one of my favourite places to go. To arrive at TV Centre in a taxi, be let in through the barrier by the gateman, then to be allowed into the inner sanctum of the building by the receptionist, to be escorted up to the *Top of the Pops* studio or the dressing rooms – well it literally was another of my dreams come true.

I seemed to have the run of the place, eventually. Slade liked to eat in the BBC canteen so we'd spend the odd half hour talking over egg and chips or a cheese sandwich and tea. Then I'd go into the studio with them (or whoever I had come to interview) and become one of the dancers. Mum would sit at home in Buckingham and watch the screen every Thursday looking out for me and would ring the next day if she had spotted me. In later years the programme was pre-recorded, but in the early days it was always live.

A few years ago, there was a retrospective on TV about the *Top of the Pops* heyday, and I happened to switch it on. There was Julie Webb, being interviewed about those days, and then there was a clip of, if I remember, Edison Lighthouse, and there was this girl in a greeny-patterned mini dress, dancing in quite a lithe, watchable sort of way, with long, long hair – and then I realised it was me.

The young enthusiasm, the sheer abandon, the youthful suppleness of the body, the way I was, it made me feel wistful. Sad. And rather old. Which of course I am now.

After the show, we would usually go up to the BBC bar where there were always familiar faces. The girls from Pan's People, whom I also interviewed in their dressing rooms several times in 1971 and 1972, would arrive and we'd stand by the bar chatting. Within minutes, a large crowd of male BBC employees would all decide that they needed a drink, so that they could come and have a closer inspection of the lovely Ruth, Dee Dee, Babs and co. I was prepared to hate Babs, because she was the sexiest, blondest, poutiest one – but she turned out to be quite shy and also very likeable. Why she ended up with that Robert Powell, who once played Jesus Christ in a TV mini-series, and who was one of the most pompous actors I ever did interview, I'll never know.

There was a large TV screen to one side of the BBC bar and in mid-November I sat there and watched the Miss World competition with Pan's People. It was the year that some of the first gay protesters – led by Peter Tatchell – held an alternative pageant outside the Albert Hall, with drag queen contestants called names like Miss Used and Miss Treated.

This later made the BBC news, which we also watched on the same TV before heading home. Protests like these – and the previous year when eggs had been thrown at Bob Hope during the contest by women's libbers – were the first rumblings that Miss World's days were numbered, but I always loved its naffness, and its glitz and ridiculousness. Just like the annual Eurovision song contest, it had always been around and you couldn't imagine a time without it.

So when, a week or two later, I received a phone call from Mecca, the entertainment company with Eric and Julia Morley at the helm, which ran the Miss World, I was intrigued.

They wanted me to be one of the four judges at the Mecca/Coca Cola Freestyle disco dancing championships at the Empire Ballroom, Leicester Square early in December. What my qualifications for this were, I am not too sure – as nobody at Mecca had ever seen me dancing, or checked out my credentials in the field of dance, or indeed, as a judge of anything at all.

But they did want me, and of course I accepted. And it was a fabulous '70s evening from start to finish – pure disco, pure over the top. The Jackson Five, The Sweet, Shocking Blue (remember 'Venus'?), T.Rex, Spirit in the Sky – these were the people, this was the music the sixteen or so young, crazily dressed couples were dancing to.

Julia Morley sent a limo for me and was there to meet me in the foyer. The other judges were Douggie Squires (choreographer of the New Generation TV dance troupe), Peter Denyer of *Please Sir!,* and Jack Wild, the actor from the huge hit movie *Oliver!* who was a great guy and whom I had met before. Mrs Morley was a quite formidable woman both to look at – very tall, with very dark hair piled up on her head, the highest heels – and in manner. She read us the riot act – I mean rules – and for a moment Jack and I felt like naughty schoolchildren but I thought it was great because I'd seen her behaving in exactly the same manner regularly like clockwork each year on my TV and now here she was, doing it to me! What fabulous, fabulous fun!

Jack and I had plenty to drink backstage in the green room and when the competition began were slightly horrified to find that we were expected to walk around among the disco dancers on the floor, marking them as we went. No *Strictly Come Dancing* row of comfy chairs and a desk for us, then.

I was having quite a job standing upright, let alone walking among the contestants, and was at one point nearly knocked flying by a particularly exuberant couple whom, of course, I immediately gave nil points to on my scorecard. There is nothing better for the ego of a 22-year-old than to sit in judgement on her peers in front of a cheering audience. 'Oh, I don't like that one's trousers, I'll knock them out … oh, just look at the hairdo on her, she's got to go …'.

Nowadays I watch TV talent contests and know just how those judges feel, how smug and untouchable they are. The contestants' lives in your hands – what a great feeling for an egomaniac. I have no idea whether the best couple won – I very much doubt it, we judges were all so busy trying to stand upright, being knocked over, and clocking the clothes that I think it very likely the best couple went out, first round. Never mind, I expect they got over it.

seven

To Reach the Unreachable Star

1972

Doctor Who … *Steptoe and Son* … the New Seekers at Eurovision … *The Generation Game* … *Doomwatch* … *Crossroads* … *The Godfather* … Alex Comfort's *The Joy of Sex* … *Columbo* … loon pants … *Cosmopolitan* magazine … Gilbert O' Sullivan and 'Claire' … 'Puppy Love' … it's got to be 1972.

I don't know if I really wanted to die, I just wanted things to change, that's why I took the overdose of aspirin last week. That's why I ended up in hospital in Oxford, having my stomach pumped, and feeling like an idiot when I came round.

All I wanted was to go back to Witney Grammar School and my friends, and not have to go to this horrid Bicester Grammar School any more. I hate it and everybody hates me, everybody's already got their friends and I'm so miserable and lonely I could cry … and often do. Bicester bloody Grammar School. Everyone is ignoring me or bullying me or laughing at me but Mum says I've got to go back anyway on Monday because there's nowhere else to go. So I've got to suffer for another two years and taking the aspirins was a complete waste of time, and I feel peculiar and weak as well.

Anyway, at least it's still only Friday. It's good to sit here with Dad in front of the TV. The coal fire's bright in the grate, the curtains are drawn, the world is shut out and it's just me, him and Andy Williams.

I love The Andy Williams Show. It means the weekend is ahead which is one good reason to love it, but I'd love it anyway. When the parents decided to get back together again for a trial run last year – 1963 – they found this old house in Weston-on-the-Green and the TV's become my new best friend.

Mum's gone to visit her friend Mrs Hill, like she usually does at the weekends. That's ok. Dad can cook, and we both like to sit here and relax. The weekend starts with the fab new show *Ready Steady Go!* on a Friday teatime. Keith Fordyce, well he's a bit old-fashioned, but that Cathy McGowan is good and they often have The Beatles or Billy J. Kramer on. The Andy Williams Show is usually on just before bed.

On Saturday, after Dad comes back from the pub and the betting shop, it will be wrestling with Giant Haystacks and Big Daddy, compèred by Kent Walton in the afternoon, and then *Juke Box Jury* with David Jacobs, another of my favourites (the show, not him, I think he looks supercilious) and *Thank Your Lucky Stars*, with Brian Matthew or Pete Murray. Sometimes they'll have Billy Fury on which makes it even more special. Sundays – they're no use. *Sing Something Simple* – ghastly. Nothing to watch on TV, except perhaps *Sunday Night at the London Palladium*, just homework and dreading going back to that place tomorrow.

Dad's mother, Grannie Carlisle, died just a few months ago and so he got some money from the sale of her things, and before that he sold off our house in Banbury, what was left after the mortgage, and now he's selling bits and pieces of the furniture and nick nacks in this house, so he hasn't run up any debt again. But he's been made redundant from his job as a telephone sales rep so things aren't looking good. Dad's promised Mum that he doesn't gamble but if he doesn't, why does he go to the betting shop? But these weekends, we kind of ignore all that and we get on fine, my Dad and I.

Andy Williams – he is so restful, so relaxing. He smiles and I almost believe everything can be ok. He's got such a gorgeous voice – and although he's probably at least 30 or even older, and I'm only 14, I think I quite fancy him though I wouldn't want to admit that to anyone. I wonder what he looks like in real life? I wonder what colour his hair is? And then he has those cute little Osmond Brothers on; they are so sweet but you wouldn't want to admit that to anyone either. I wonder what they'll do when they grow up?

I can remember the day now, in June 1965 after finishing my O levels, running away from that hated school down the driveway, chucking my hated brown beret in the ditch on the way home. Even now, if I ever catch sight of schoolchildren wearing brown uniform, I shiver and have to look away.

In summer 1972 I was to find out, close up, what colour Andy Williams' hair was in real life, and in the same year, I was to find out what the Osmonds were doing now they were growing up.

I also met and interviewed, in no particular order, Slade (four times), Cilla Black, Rick Nelson, Gene Pitney (twice), Jack Jones, Neil Diamond, Johnny Nash, Glen Campbell (aiming on that day for the title of World's Dumbest Celebrity), Anne Murray, The Sweet, The Drifters, Jerry Lee Lewis, Jonathan King, The Temptations, Mama Cass, Sacha Distel, José Feliciano, Neil Sedaka, Rick Wakeman, Michael Jackson, Peter Skellern, Tony Christie and many others.

→ Holding my
14th birthday
present at the
Hill's house
In Botley,
Oxford. That's
my brother
Rob, who had
come to visit.
I wore a tooth
brace but still
managed a
smile.

→ Billy Fury,
complete with
'bird poo hat'
and me age
16, outside
the stage
door of the
New Theatre,
Oxford, 1965.

Hi there, friends. Well, the summer may be drawing to a close, but those knock-out 208 shows seem to go on forever. Read on to find out all about them. . . .

TUES 12th SEPT

Mike Hazlewood.

AND, we're off, as usual, with my Pick of the Week spot, in which the honours this time round go to singer/songwriter Mike Hazlewood for his newie *Fine White Stallion*.

It's a beautiful ballad which tells the story of a guy who has nothing going for him, and is asking his horse to carry him to a new life.

This song has a message and I'm sure that after a couple of listens you'll get hooked on the simple but thoughtful way Mike sings it.

There's a certain charm about the whole thing—and keep an ear open, 'cos the disc will be popping up on those 208 shows quite a lot.

WED 13th SEPT

th SEPT

THURS 1

HAD the ple meeting Jack Oliv together make

↑ Radio Luxembourg's Doug Perry was my first (disastrous) date in London – here's his page in *Fab* at the time.

→ Me doing my first modelling session for *Fabulous*, complete with Biba feather boa, summer 1967.

1969

WITH KENNEDY BROWN

immy Justice locks in again

← Billy Fury's brother, Jason Eddie (Albert Wycherley) makes it on to the pages of *Fab* in 1969.

● American West Coast group Blood, Sweat and Tears created such a stir with their debut album that the record company has issued a single from it. It's called *You Made Me So Very Happy* and it's brilliant (CBS).
● Founder Shadow member Hank Marvin goes solo with the catchy guitar instrumental *Goodnight, Dick* (Columbia).
● Remember *Do Wah Diddy Diddy*, a hit five years ago for Manfred Mann? Now the original version, by the Exciters, has been re-issued (United Artists)
● Also worth spinning: *I'll Catch The Sun* by Kathy Kirby (Columbia), *Plastic Man* by the Kinks (Pye), *In A Moment Of Madness* by the Flower Pot Men (Deram), *Yesterday's Sunshine* by John Walker (Philips) and *Moonlight Brings Memories* by Clinton Ford (Pye).

GER Jimmy Jus- was top of the ops five years ago a string of hit including *Spanish* and *When My Smiling*. n came the beat boom and, according to Jimmy, "the ass went sour on and I became de-sed with it". ork became scarce faced with a weekly of £150 to keep his ing group together he possibility of his ngs going down the , he decided to showbiz.

reatest

went into the pro-ty business, with the casional singing earance in clubs to his tonsils in ge. recently, Jimmy ar-ged a house deal a man who later

met recording manager Dick Rowe and men-tioned he had run into the one-time pop idol.

"He was one of the greatest singers we've ever had," said Dick. "I always wondered what happened to him. I'd love to see him back on disc."

Cautious

Dick contacted Jimmy, persuaded him to return to the studios and now he reappears this week with a beaty, Country-and-Western ballad called *I'm Running Out Of Time* (Decca).

Jimmy is now 27 and is cautiously planning a comeback into the pop business.

"But," he said, "I'll only give up 90 per cent of my time to it. After all, I still have a lot of property interests to take care of."

After hearing his

Jimmy Justice . . . the pop business went sour on him

latest disc, I wonder why he ever left the music scene. He could well have a hit on his hands.

JASON'S CHASING BIG BROTHER

JASON EDDIE is making a bid for the charts with a strong ballad called *Heart And Soul* . . . and he's hoping it will set him on the same road to pop success as big brother Billy Fury.

Jason is 21 and started in showbiz three years ago while working variously as a butcher, baker, driver, lumberjack and TV salesman.

Last year he turned full-time pro-fessional and promoted his own road show, *The Jason Eddie Rock And Roll Show*, followed by a tour of Northern clubs as a solo singer.

He sings on the Tangerine label.

JEFF FINDS A LONELY GIRL

JEFF KANE makes his debut with *Pretty Young Lady* (Tangerine), written by Ray Cameron and Alan Hawkshaw, inspired by Carol White's character in the film *Poor Cow*.

The song tells the story of a young girl from Battersea, called Jenny, who was ten and neglected by her father when she was ten and able to leave home.

Jeff, 22, from East Molesey, Surrey, started singing with his own package show. He took it to Germany, Italy, North Africa and Cyprus.

On his return he had a short stint in Jeff and Jon.

Pop LP

ENGELBERT, of course, features Mr. Humperdinck singing a lush selection of superior ballads helped along by big-sounding orchestral arrangements. Titles include *Through The Eyes Of Love*, *The Way It Used To Be* and *Les Bicyclettes de Paris*. Hump is in great voice and it's bound to be a best-seller (Decca)

Jazz choice

THE Count Basie orchestra has been turning out a lot of strange-sounding records, but *Basie—Straight Ahead* is their latest, is strictly powerful, instrumental jazz by the most swinging t

→ Hal Carter's baby's christening with Billy Fury on the right and me in a stupid hat right behind him, Jimmy Campbell top left and Gordon Coxhill from *NME* centre back.

← One month into my job as ed's sec, I find myself in the *Daily Mirror*. But I've morphed into Judy Wallace.

↑ Some Gorgeous Girls (and I use that term loosely) with Tom Jones at the Royal Albert Hall (that's me on his left).

BRITAIN'S GORGEOUS GIRLS

EVEN the rain cannot dampen the spirits of Britain's Gorgeous Girls. For the moment it stops, there they are . . . still smil-

ing and still looking perfectly lovely. They do say that every cloud has a silver lining. And proving the point in London yesterday

was Judy Wallace, 18, who takes notes as a secretary in the City. Watch the *Mirror* as we take note of more gorgeous girls.

→ *Fab* reports my meeting with Tom Jones; my old hero Richard Chamberlain has to make do with a smaller photo.

CHAMBERLAIN NEW B.B.C. SER

BEE GEES BIG FUTURE

STILL celebrating their reprieve The Bee Gees are getting down to planning their future.

It's only a short time since the Home Office told the two Australian boys that they could work in England indefinitely, and already a new album, three tours and a film are being planned.

They are planning a terrific three-week tour of Britain, probably in March, and hope to tour Australia and America for about five weeks in the new year.

They are also discussing the possibility of making the film *Lord Kitchener's Little Drummer Boys* in the spring.

Their next single *World* is due for release any minute, and their album *Horizontal* is due for release before Christmas. All the fourteen tracks were written by The Bee Gees.

Massachusetts has just won the boys their first silver disc.

Hollies Societie Disc

THE HOLLIES' first-ever record production, *Bird Has Flown* by The Societie, has been set for 17th November issue, on the Deram label.

The Societie is a teenage group from Glasgow, and this is their first record.

Organist Dave Dougall wrote the song, and the group also includes a singer called Rubbie Burns, a drummer named Smiler Ferate, and a girl guitarist, Susie Struthers.

November Sparklers

CARNABY SPARKLERS are coming in. Definitely not a group but new pop nail lacquers in gold or silver.

Not dense metallic colour but sparkly bits suspended in colourless varnish.

For party glitter, model girls choose one coat of varnish—foils at once. For colourful sparkle, one coat of either over usual pink or sheeny lacquer.

In the shops late November (Mintex, 5s. 3d. a time) for all razzle-dazzle dollies.

FABULOUS DRESS

OUR special £2 dress offer is going like a bomb. Favourite colours, so far are orange,

GOOD news for fans of the of Blair Hospital, Richard Richard himself will be arrivi any day now to begin working he B.B.C. 2 colour television series.

Dr. K to the self, i sode s James trait of

He pla Touchet TB. Rich play is S Richard U.S. at British ago, but any tin recording Decemb This lo looker is losing hi is taking to cultiv tone. It the same Sean Co accent. Richar settling his home he spend New Yo This r work r Richard

FAE Neai

ONL\ before A-Z of page boo This w centre of take our 20, 21 an before, cr and fold marked.

FAB Editor's Secretary Judy Wills was chosen as one of the *Daily Mirror's* Gorgeous Girls, and here's lovely Judy (right) with gorgeous Tom Jones at the *Daily Mirror's* Gorgeous Girls Golden Gala at The Royal Albert Hall. Altogirl!

●● FILM SPOT ●●

EXCITING ROBBERY

IN 1963 a gang of men held up the 6.50 p.m. mail train from Glasgow to Euston and got away with over £1 million.

The press immediately chris-

mendous attention to detail. The robbery itself will have you edgy on your seats, and then just as exciting is the methodical, patient way in which James Booth and his fellow cops set out to track down and capture most of the crooks. The photography is always shot from the most dramatic angles and the cast, although not particularly well-known, are fine in every way. Don't miss *Robbery*.

B SAYS

LISHED THIS MONTH in sian for the first time is the plish translation of Russia's -selling monthly digest, UTNIK (priced three shill-), a fascinating look at life in s from space to sport, to psychology.

NOVEMBER TNIK includes a highly ing study of youth in called *Portrait of a Gener-*based on a poll among s from the age of fourteen enty-three throughout

Sociologist Vladimir brilliantly assesses the s given by young people d questions as "What you most like to possess?" What is your attitude to the generation?"

HUNDRED boys and who answered the latter question, 70 per cent said they in as well with their parents. typical answer: "I spect the older generation. They can teach us to be real eople, to live, build and win enough."

EVIEW of the remainder, who didn't get on with their parents, has had a familiar ring about it: key are too fond of lecturing us d propounding truths we now already. Our generation ceives its education earlier than they did. What our fathers did at learn until they were twenty, we get to know by the time we re sixteen."

IST OF THE ANSWERS, in ct, were remarkably similar to ose given by FAB readers in sponse to our WE WANT TO NOW ABOUT YOU ques- ionaire.

d about their greatest fears, largest group (33-8 per cent) the arrival of war. Other fears ere loneliness and indifference. his tallies exactly with the sponse from YOU.

THER SIMILARITY was e question of how one would end a suddenly acquired for- ne. As in your answers, the ajority would "treat" their rents, and another many top would elect for travel. Only a 12 per cent merely old spend the money purely n luxury items for themselves, he fast cars and tape recorders re high on their shopping list.

SSIAN YOUNGSTERS em to popular music more an any other kind; want rama and happiness rather an material possessions. They ant peace on earth, and most first to their parents for dvice.

ming up his findings, Vladimir niner says of Russia's young: bout being scornful of aternal goods, they give greater ference to moral values. They concerned about the fate of e world?"

generation not so very removed from our own, fter all.

→ Groovy Girl fashion in *Fab*, part one – my first appearance in the magazine. See bottom left, it mentions me ...

↓ At the 'Gorgeous Girls' Gala, Royal Albert Hall, October 1967.

→ Part two of Groovy Girl.

→ I share the front cover of *The Sunday Mirror* with Engelbert Humperdinck (me far right).

Sunday Mirror

6d October 1, 1967 No. 233

What has Engelbert got to do with

THE NAKED APE?

← A spot of modelling for *Fab* with Elaine Paige.

PLUM CRAZY

You always suspected we wuz a bit nutty, didn't you? Well, now we've gone and put it in writing: we iz plum crazy! Plums may give you a pain in your tum, but they have been the inspiration of the year for our designers. Everybody's plumming it! So just in case you give a plum for being in the 'in' colour we've photographed a few of the choicest (as the greengrocer would say!).
by HEATHER KIRBY. Photographs by FRANK BUCK

2nd SEPTEMBER, 1967

Fabulous 208 FALL GUYS

EVERY WEEK THE MONKEES AND GEORGE BEST WRITE FOR YOU
DOUBLE PAGE COLOUR PIC OF THE BEATLES ● KING SIZE COLOUR PIN-UPS OF ● PINK FLOYD ● MIKE NESMITH ● BOB RANDUM ● BRIAN WILSON ● TINA AUMONT ● ALSO YOUR COMPLETE RADIO LUXEMBOURG PROGRAMMES FROM 29th AUGUST TU 4th SEPTEMBER.

→ *Fab* 'Fall Guys' cover September 1967 featuring Keith Richards, Mick Jagger, Donovan, Scott Walker, *The Man from U.N.C.L.E.*, Rudolf Nureyev, Sandie Shaw, Mohammad Ali (Cassius Clay as was) and The Monkees.

↑ *Fab* October 1967 cover featuring The Monkees.

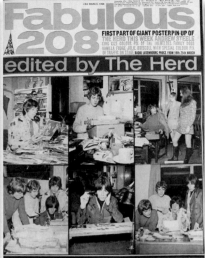

↑ *Fab* cover, 1968, featuring The Herd – Peter Frampton top centre (and self with office junior Sue, top right).

↑ My moment of fame – on the cover of *Honey* magazine which was, at the time, 'young, gay and get-ahead'.

→ JW and the lovely Anne Wilson, doing that coy girls modelling thing for a *Fab* fashion feature.

WELCOME TO AB-208 19

You are now an honorary member of the Fab Gang . . . who compiled this book. You'll see that we've left spaces on some of the pages for you to do your bit.

Now meet the Gang . . .

That's me in the first office with my secretary, Judy. (She has gorgeous red hair.)

Office 2 is the lair of our smooth Assistant Ed., John. Tripping through his office is Twiggy type Sue, FAB's Girl Friday.

Heather, the Fashion Ed., is the dishy dolly in the maxi and Sally, who writes the Beauty, is in the bell-bottoms. The office loaded with letters belongs to Cliff and Anne, our Letterbox experts.

Art Ed., Tom, rules the roost in the Art Room with Jenny (very mini skirted) and Val (mad keen Tony Blackburn fan) to help. Writers are June (the chief one), Anne (who looks after TV and films), Pam (our newshound), Chris (gossip expert) and Doug who brings all the news from Luxembourg.

Ann organises Peter (FAB's photographer) and is in charge of the Picture Desk.

Mo sees all the pages safely to the printers and checks everything is present and correct.

So now on· with FAB-208 1969 . . . and remember you can meet the gang every week in FABULOUS-208.

Betty (The Ed.)

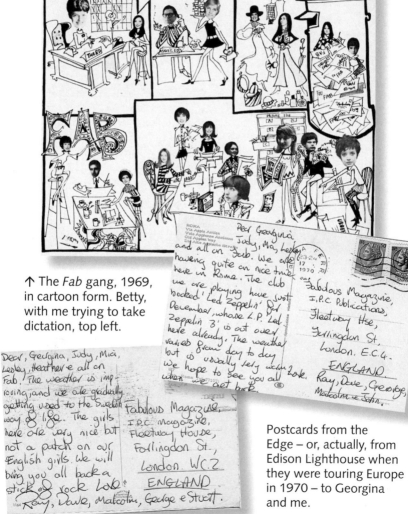

↑ The *Fab* gang, 1969, in cartoon form. Betty, with me trying to take dictation, top left.

Postcards from the Edge – or, actually, from Edison Lighthouse when they were touring Europe in 1970 – to Georgina and me.

→ *Fab* gang, 1970; me top left looking miserable, Julie Webb left of centre, Betty Hale centre.

meet the Fab gang

May we introduce ourselves? We're the FAB Gang, who produced this book and you can check all our names on the chart.

John is Assistant Ed. and general trouble-shooter. Tom, with Christine, Dave and Roy produced the art work and layouts. Janet, Anne G. and Robbie checked all the facts and figures

and saw that everything made sense! Ann Moore, Picture Ed., lined up the people for the photos and organised Roger, our photographer. Heather did the fashion and Sally the beauty. Anne W., Julie and Pam wrote a lot of the words. Judith, Ed's Secretary, and Lorraine, our girl Friday, efficiently kept us all organised.

Cliff and Valli compiled the Birthday Calendar.

Meet the FAB Gang every week in FABULOUS 208, the best weekly there is—in our opinion! Love,

Betty

1. Judith Wills
2. Roger Brown
3. Pamela Townsend
4. John Fearn
5. Roy Coleman
6. Dave Rowley
7. Anne Gillingham
8. Brian Thomas
9. Robbie Martin
10. Christine Wiskin
11. Sally Cork
12. Clifford Jacob
13. Anne Wilson
14. Ann Moore
15. Heather Kirby
16. Lorraine Wright
17. Janet Crumbie
18. Valli Bond
19. Julie Webb
20. Betty Hale

→ Tony Prince, Radio Luxembourg DJ, and I having a bit of 'fun' at the 208 London headquarters.

↑ Kid Jensen and me having a reflective moment in his room in Luxembourg town, 1970.

→ Les Gray of Mud and me at some PR bash at Brands Hatch motor racing circuit.

← The *Fab* Gang circa 1971; me bottom right, looking suicidal, probably hungover. Georgina Mells and Betty Hale are in the centre.

FABGANG1971

This is the laughing, stamping, taping, writing, clicking, snapping, drawing, designing, persuading crowd of people who put this book together. It's the same team that gets together FAB 208 each week. In detail, we are: (starting at the top, l. to r.) Richard Stone (chief sub), . Reeve (art

4

NEWS OF THE WORLD, September 12, 1971 3

WANTED

Britain's sexiest girl!

■ DO YOU KNOW a marvellously sexy girl, as yet unfiscovered?

"If you do, you can win her—and the companion of her choice—the holiday of a lifetime. All you have to do is to send us her photograph to enter her in this year's most exciting competition.

WIN THE HOLIDAY OF A LIFETIME

and address, on the back.

And the prize for Britain's Sexiest Girl when we find her

Anyone

We believe that Britain is full of fantastically sexy girls and we're looking for the sexiest one of all.

The holiday of a lifetime. She will be selected away from Britain on a BOAC Earthshaker holiday all the way to Montego Bay in sunny Jamaica.

There she'll spend two weeks in the luxurious Holiday Inn hotel, and sunning herself on Jamaica's golden beaches.

Panel

If you're the competition's the contest, you'll be there too. If you're a £100 competition prize?

We'll be publishing pictures of the finalists in the News of the World, and appointing a panel of authoritative judges to decide the Sexiest Girl in Britain.

Plans and your entries to:

"Britain's Sexiest Girl Competition," 26, Bouverie Street, London, EC4Y 0AD. Closing date Sept 26. Hurry, hurry!

No negligence in boys hostel—MP

AN INVESTIGATION into a hostel whose deputy warden was jailed for indecently assaulting boys was found there was no negligence.

Factory blasted

→ Self, complete with best-ironed hair, as photographed by Beverly Goodway for *News of the World*.

← Leonard Nimoy and I chat during a coffee break on the set of *Catlow* in Almeria, Spain, May 1971.

→ Nimoy and me having a rest after the walk to the top of the fort in Almeria.

↓ Postcard to my mother from Almeria 1971, mentioning actor Yul Brynner as a 'big-headed cow'.

→ I write Slade's 'life story' for *Fab* – bottom right, Noddy Holder and I chat.

↓ My invitation to Mecca! Or, at least, the letter from them inviting me to be a judge at their disco-dancing competition.

→ A page from my diary for 1972 – Slade, Mama Cass, Sacha Distel, Johnny Nash … and the dentist.

← At the Dorchester hotel in February 1972 interviewing David Cassidy, complete with his favourite yeti boots.

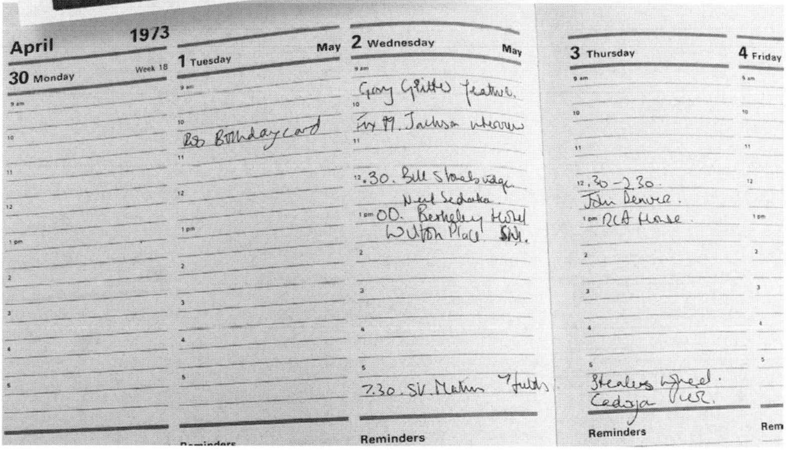

April	1973						
30 Monday	Week 18	**1** Tuesday	May	**2** Wednesday	May	**3** Thursday	**4** Friday

(handwritten diary entries:)

Wed 2 May: Gary Glitter feature. Fix 99 Jackson interview. 12.30. Bill Shoalsridge Neil Sedaka. 1 pm OO. Berkeley Hotel Wilton Place SW1. 2.30 SV Mahan Fields

Thurs 3 May: 12.30–2.30. John Denver. 1 pm RCA House. Stealers Wheel. Cadoza Visit.

Tues 1 May: R.O. Birthday card

↑ A diary page from 1973.

→ Interviewing Donny Osmond – probably summer 1972.

← The IOU I received from Andy Williams after I gave him my cigarette lighter. The signature at the top was mine, and the one underneath was his – but he wrote my name instead! He was a bit out of it at the time.

recieved lighter from 24 Wilton Pl. July 14, 1972

Signature _Judith E. Wills_
                Judith Wills

→ *Fab* competition winner Judi and I at Disneyland, LA, 1973.

↓ Donny Osmond sings to Judi in Las Vegas while Betty Hale (left) and I look on (Osmond brothers legs in the background).

→ One of the *Fab* Dream Come True features, with David Essex and reader Karen.

Karen Gill nearly passed out when we phoned her and said, "We'd like to make your dream come true!" Karen who lives in New Malden, Surrey, said her dream was to meet and spend an evening with DAVID ESSEX, star of *That'll be the Day* and *Godspell*.

Dream Come True

My name ... KAREN GILL
Address ... GEORGE ROAD
NEW MALDEN, SURREY, KT3-6GU.

KAREN MEETS DAVID

WELL no sooner asked than granted and after we'd phoned David to fix a suitable evening and after Karen had recovered from the shock there were only a couple of days to go to D (David!) Day!

Karen arrived at the FAB offices on THE day looking pretty calm, considering! We fixed her up with a nice photo for David to sign, and also decided that it would be a great idea to take along the tape recorder and record a conversation with David as an extra-special souvenir of the evening.

By the time we reached the stage door of Wyndham's Theatre, where Karen was to meet David, she was beginning to get nervous. Then before she knew it we were in David's dressing room, and there HE was — all twinkling eyes and very friendly. Soon Karen realised that she had had no need to be nervous 'cos David put her at ease right away. He gave Karen a huge Pace poster of himself which he signed, plus a copy of his new record, *Rock On*. While the tape recorder was on, David chatted away about the show, his career, and so on. Then, in a daze, Karen left David to prepare for the show. "Come back later!" he said. "I'd be pleased to see you!"

Uh, isn't he lovely!" said Karen, as she had a meal. "But

Above: Karen won't wash that cheek for ages now that David's giving her a welcome kiss!

Right: she's very pleased with her specially-autographed copy of Rock On.

Left: Nearly time for the show to begin but Karin's still in a dream!

Below: David gets involved in a chat with Karen and all the time the tape is going so Karen will always remember what he said!

↑ Keith Moon doing his Noel Coward impression backstage. Do I spot my handbag in the background?

↑ Alan Osmond signs autographs for fans at London Heathrow in 1973. That's me on the right, waiting to join him in the Osmond limo to London.

↑ The Moon lets rip on stage, body art well hidden – for the moment.

→ A trip to The Derby with Mud in June 1975 just before I left *Fab*.

MUD

Ray's being taken for a ride!

All aboard!

Not quite your size, Dave.

Two to Epsom please!

Dave's on to a winner!

Signing a paper plate.

On the merry way home

Lots of love –
We'll miss you
like anything.
As ever Betty.

But will I ever forgive Pauline
to bring the breakfast in the tent
at 11.30?!
Happy Early Listings
Pauline x

Lots of Luck in all you do
The Fab Gang will be missing you –
Your brilliant features, 208
Your matchless copy (always late!)
Hope your days are nice and sunny.
Full of fun and lots of money!
May you find the things you seek
And Have a FAB Time Every Week!

← Goodbye, *Fab*! My leaving card.

Gene Pitney was another of the stars who could have counted me as a true fan, a few years earlier. I went to the New Theatre, Oxford, to see him perform with my friend Cookie, and collected all his records. How well I remember my brother Rob saying 'How on earth can you go and see him – he's dreadful! He sounds like a wailing tom cat!'

When I met him – at the Westbury Hotel in the West End, on 28 February 1972, I was delighted to find that he seemed a genuinely friendly and funny person. However, of course during interviews it wasn't always easy to tell what someone was really like. A year or two later I met and interviewed another huge pop star more than once, who came from my early hometown of Banbury. I thought he was the most lovely man you could meet, and said so in print. I also admired him for his charitable work for children's charities. Only trouble was, his name was Gary Glitter.

Another huge celeb who always seemed ok to me – if a bit weird – was Jimmy Savile, which all goes to show what a bad judge of character I was, as well as being such a bad judge of who was going to be a big star and who wasn't.

That said, I do think Pitney was a great guy and all through the years I haven't heard any dodgy stories about him at all.

Another early hero of mine, based purely on the fact that he had (from what I could tell of the photos printed of him in *Roxy* magazine and *Marilyn* magazine) beautiful blue eyes and fantastic curly Elvis-like lips, and sang cutely on a single called 'Hello Mary Lou' (coincidentally, written by Gene Pitney) was Ricky Nelson. Sadly when I finally got to meet him in February during his career-revival attempt through country music and a single called 'Garden Party', he seemed somewhat lacking in the brains and charisma departments and then later, when I dragged The Boss along to the Albert Hall to see him in concert (yes, by this time we were getting rather lovely-dovey again) that February, he was dire. So dire, we left early, with my full consent. And that was the end of my love affair with the Nelson, who was killed in a plane crash in 1985.

Have I mentioned Tony Blackburn yet in this book? No – I thought not. I don't know why, as Tony was always popping up in our lives. By 1972 he was perhaps the top Radio 1 DJ, with masses of confidence on air and a cheery chappie radio persona which neatly summed up everything about the bubblegum days of the early '70s and my kind of ridiculous pop. In real life, although he could be like that, he seemed to be awash with self-doubt and lack of self-belief.

For a while, he had a crush on Julie Webb. We didn't see that much of each other by now because she was working at *NME*. But one day we both arrived at a lunchtime press performance by The Carpenters at the old Talk of the Town off Leicester Square. Karen and Richard Carpenter were selling shedloads of albums and the place was packed out. As a dinner-dance/ theatre venue, it was cabaret-style seating at long tables, and sitting next to me and opposite Julie, was Tony.

Blackburn was upset at his lack of success with the ladies, and wanted to talk about it. He'd just met a girl called Tessa but didn't know whether she liked him or not and wanted minute detail from me on how he should behave to gain best advantage. As the gig went on, Tony talked and talked and talked, and at the end of it I felt wrung out but quite flattered that he'd chosen to tell his troubles to me.

As I left, he was chatting to Julie. And next time I spoke to her, I found out that he'd done the same number on her, at equal length – with the difference that at the end, he asked her out. She didn't go. Of course.

We all put up with Tony, because although he was a bit of an idiot in some respects, he was a lovable idiot, always.

Around this time there was something much more important brewing – the visit to the UK by David Cassidy.

By the time he arrived – on 7 February (a fact recorded in big letters in my diary, almost as if I was impressed by this myself) – he was the biggest star, in teenybopper terms, that the UK had ever seen. Through his role as Keith Partridge in the TV show *The Partridge Family*, and a string of hit records, despite being no great singer, as far as I could tell, he was massive – and the crowds at Heathrow and the hysterical fans who followed him round everywhere that week proved it. I firmly believe that if you want to be a teen idol, you can get a long, long way on great hair, a wide smile and a good set of teeth. As Mr Bieber knows today.

I was with Cassidy most of the week, and quite puffed up with a sense of my own importance as I was not only the official *Fab* representative but had also been commissioned by a US magazine called *Star* to be their UK correspondent for the Cassidy tour.

On the 8th there was a bus organised to take David and selected press, me included, round all the tourist spots of London for photo opportunities – but sadly we only got as far as Buckingham Palace and had to pack it in because the weather was dire and David didn't want to get wet and cold.

On Thursday 10th I had my proper private interview with him at the Dorchester in his suite and had to shove hundreds of girls, who were crowding the outside, out of the way in order to get there. Even after all these years on *Fab* I still found this something of a buzz. I guess it made me feel glamorous, that old stardust rubbing off on little old me again. The fact that they all hated me for going to the one place they wanted to go – David Cassidy's bedroom – kind of didn't matter.

In truth, David Cassidy was quite unexceptional in every way, as far as I could tell, except that he had quite heavy pancake make-up on, which, in those days, wasn't the norm apart from glam rockers on stage. This was, I daresay, an attempt to mask the spots which had broken out on his face due, no doubt, to the stress of the tour. The famous smile didn't show itself a lot except when the photographer, David Porter, turned his camera on him; he was a bit grumpy and a bit taking himself seriously, and while he wasn't the worst person I've ever interviewed he was not easy.

But hey, I went away and wrote how lovely he was, because the truth wasn't what the teenyboppers or the pop magazine editors wanted to hear, everything had to be wonderful.

A year or two later it turned out that at the time the boy was seriously depressed about his career and looking for some proper meaning in life; he quit the business and his demeanour all that week made sense. He was just being truthful. He couldn't pretend.

Except, of course, he was supposed to be an actor.

Mind you, he never won any Oscars. And I can understand that.

1972 was also the year I was finally to meet The Osmonds. In March 1972 they had another minor hit in the UK charts, 'Down by the Lazy River'. Meanwhile in America they were doing much better.

One way or another (probably via Bill Sammeth's powers of persuasion) they had managed to get a spot on our Royal Variety Performance in May. The group used the opportunity to spend several days in the UK doing press, radio and whatever TV they could get, which, as I recall, wasn't a great deal. Thus they had to more or less make do with me – and my diary lists 'Friday 19th, Churchill Hotel, Osmonds' 'Tuesday 23rd, Churchhill Hotel, Osmonds' and 'Wednesday 24th, 2.30pm, Osmonds'.

Of all this, I recall next to nothing. I still don't think I was convinced at that stage.

By this time I had finished with doing beauty at *Fab* for good, and not a moment too early. The TV and film coverage had gone to Georgina, and I was concentrating virtually 100 per cent on music (loosely speaking, as much of it was by no means actual music as you may know it) which suited me well. I still had my coterie of music journalist friends – Julie, Richard Green (The Beast) from the *NME*, Nigel Hunter, who by this time was working for *Music Business Weekly*, and Roy Carr. Between us we always had a huge choice of freebies.

One of our favourite haunts was the murkily lit, smoke-infested Ronnie Scott's club in Wardour Street. I don't remember ever once paying to get in, probably because there seemed to be a music business reception, or a showcase for a particular artist or band – Long John Baldry was one of the best – there virtually every night. In March we watched Slade launch their album *Slade, Alive!* which was to stay in the UK album charts for over a year, at the club.

Ronnie Scott would get up on stage at the end of the reception and after a couple of polite attempts to get us to leave, would yell out, 'Fuck off, the lot of you ...'. In those days, hearing someone say those words still had an element of shock, unlike today. If we didn't fancy fucking off, we'd just stay on all evening. But Ronnie didn't really mind as we always ordered plenty of expensive drinks from the miniskirted girls who would roam the banks of dimly-lit tables taking our orders.

Other haunts were the Revolution club, The Speakeasy, The Marquee, Scotch of St James and The Cromwellian – but I was never a great nightclub-goer because I always used to fall asleep while all around me disco danced until dawn.

I was still living at 35 Avonmore Road – the bedsit was on the second floor and was pretty basic, with a kitchen partitioned off, a cubby hole curtained off for storage, and a room of about 18ft by 12ft containing two 2ft 6in single beds. One day in the spring of 1972 I was quite surprised when the doorbell rang and when I raced down the stairs, there, clutching a large, leather holdall was The Boss.

'I've come to stay,' he said. I was so surprised it didn't cross my mind to say 'no', so he moved into the spare bed and thus began our live-in life together. He'd moved from a swish three-bedroom apartment in De Vere Gardens, Kensington W8 to a grotty bedsit in London W14. Well, that was his choice.

One day in July an invitation arrived in the post to a press reception at The Savoy – and as soon as I looked at it I knew it was one I was not going to miss. It was for Andy Williams who was going to be based in town for a few days during a large European tour. I'd met all of my other heroes from my teenage years except Andy, so I wasn't going to let this slip by. But it was more than just ticking him off, like a trainspotter does with trains. He'd meant such a lot to me.

So at lunchtime I wandered over to The Savoy, which was only a short walk from the office on the other side of The Strand, down some stairs to the large reception room and there he was, right in front of me, it was that easy. The guy who had almost single-handedly saved my life by appearing, soothing, on TV every week when I was a depressed young teen.

He was sitting in a corner surrounded by a few journalists all scribbling notes. So I grabbed a drink and sidled over, sat down nearby and watched and listened. Trying outwardly to look cool, inwardly stomach doing somersaults because that voice was so smooth, so good to listen to, even better here in The Savoy than it had been on TV ten years or so ago. God I wished he'd start singing …

After a while, I realised he was looking at me as he was talking to one of the male journos. To run away, to blush, to ignore him or what? Well, I smiled. Just a small sort of smile, nothing too broad, I didn't want him to think I was a member of the Andy Williams fan club or anything.

I just really wanted to have his megawatt American smile all for me alone, just once. And I got it. He grinned at me and there I was, back in Weston-on-the-Green, looking at Andy Williams but this time he *was* in colour – and his hair was light brown.

I got up and walked away, and downed a couple of drinks far too quickly through nerves. On an empty stomach, the first drink went straight to my head. I seem to remember it was champagne. A few people I knew drifted in and I began talking to them.

'Aren't you going to go and ask Mr Williams a few questions?' said one.

'He'd like you.'

'Why do you say that?'

'Well, I think he likes the young ladies – and I do mean young.'

'But I'm 23!' God that's nearly middle-aged!'

'Ah but with that short skirt … and you're skinny – you could pass for 16. Today, anyway!' And he walked off, smirking.

Williams was still surrounded by press – mostly from the nationals – and I just couldn't bring myself to go and squeeze myself in and start asking teenage magazine questions, I just couldn't do it.

So as the party was nearly over anyway, I decided to call it a day and walked over towards the stairs up to the foyer. I glanced over at Andy as I went, thinking well, I've seen him – we didn't talk, but we did smile. That would have to do.

But at that moment he too got up; I heard him taking his leave of everyone and within seconds he, plus his record company minders, was also walking towards the stairs. As I climbed them, in probably the shortest miniskirt I had at the time, I was completely aware that right behind me, my Last Teen Hero was following me up the stairs and I could actually feel his eyes on my legs. I felt myself going hot and as soon as I got to the top I shot out the entrance of The Savoy and hurried back to the office.

It wasn't because of my skirt length, or the fact that the legendary Andy Williams had been looking at my legs that I had felt embarrassed – it was for the simple reason that I didn't like my legs from the knee downwards. I was kicking myself for not wearing my over-knee suede boots. But it was mid-July and in those days you just didn't do that Alexa Chung-boho-period kind of thing with your fashion. So I was quite sure that instead of admiring me and noticing me in a nice kind of way, Andy Williams had left The Savoy going, 'Oh, hell, just look at that girl's revolting legs …'.

The next day I was sitting in the office gazing out of my first-floor window at the employees of IPC going in and out of the main building on the other side of Southampton Street when the phone rang.

I picked it up and a male voice with an American accent began, 'Hi – is that Judy?'

'Yes, it's Judy Wills here.'

'Hi – it's Andy!'

That's Andy Williams voice, I thought.

'Andy who?' I said.

'Andy Williams' the voice said, sounding slightly crestfallen.

'Oh, hi Andy – how are you doing?' I said, as if a) I had been expecting his call and b) I talked to him every day.

I had finally sorted out my early telephone phobia and found it much easier to be bold and laid back on the phone than in person. God, if I could have done the Isle of Wight Festival on the phone, just think what wonderful scoops I could have got.

'Well I noticed you at The Savoy the other day and I asked who you were, so they found me your number. Hope you don't mind …'.

'No, not at all …'.

'I wondered if you'd let me take you out – I haven't much spare time, they're keeping me busy, but can we have lunch tomorrow? I could come and pick you up in the car if you give me the address.'

So I spent the next minute giving Andy Williams my work address so he could come and pick me up next day in his car and take me out.

'One o' clock then – don't be late!' said Andy Williams in his best, smiley, familiar voice, and he rang off.

Ten seconds later.

'Mum! Andy Williams just rang me. He wants to see me for lunch tomorrow. He's going to come here and pick me up!' I squeaked.

'Mum – and do you know what? He rang me and he said, "It's Andy here" and do you know what I said to him? I said, "Andy who?"'

My mother retold that story many times in the years ahead.

Well I told The Boss – who, you will recall, was by this time sharing my bedsit in West Kensington – that Andy Williams had rung me. But I didn't tell him that I was going to lunch with him. Well lunch wasn't much, was it? Lunch wasn't a date.

Could have been work, anyway. Perhaps Andy Williams wanted to tell *Fab 208* magazine all about his latest easy listening album. Perhaps Andy Williams felt that without *Fab 208* magazine his whole European tour would be as nothing.

Back at home several hours were spent trying on and discarding every outfit I had, then deciding on the one I first thought of – another mini dress, floral patterned I believe, and this time I would wear knee-high canvas boots and damn the hot weather.

Washed and ironed hair, bathed.

Next morning I was glad I wasn't a bloke because I would definitely have cut myself shaving.

And at the appointed minute, I looked out of my office window and a huge Roller was outside, and a chauffeur was getting out and making his way towards our office door. I sat and waited. A minute later the Ed's Sec arrived at my desk.

'Andy Williams is waiting for you downstairs,' she said.

'Oh, right, thanks,' I replied, all nonchalance. The second she'd gone I gathered my handbag and scooted down the stairs, only slowing down when I reached the door to the street. At this point I took a few deep breaths and forced myself to saunter out towards the roller's open rear door, as if Andy Williams came to pick me up every day of the week.

I jumped in and there he was – I'd thought perhaps he had just sent the car to get me, but no, he was doing a personal appearance for a rapt audience of one.

'We're going to have lunch at my place,' he said. 'We've got a nice house in Knightsbridge and they're doing us food. I hope you don't mind.'

And there followed some of the most surreal hours of my young life. We arrived at the address in Wilton Place, one of those classical gorgeous terraces tucked away between Sloane Street and Hyde Park Corner. Inside, a few hangers-on were sitting around drinking. I was introduced and Andy and I sat side by side on a squashy sofa tucked neatly into a recess. A couple of helpers buzzed around waiting on Mr Williams' every whim.

I can't remember what we had to eat nor exactly what we talked about but an hour or two passed with no bother, some of the time him holding my hand. Andy only left my side to go to the loo once or twice and to take occasional phone calls.

At one stage he remarked that I was uncannily like his great friend Shirley MacLaine both to look at and in personality.

'That's why I noticed you,' he said. 'She's one of my favourite, best friends.'

I told him that was interesting because my mother used to tell me I looked like her as a kid.

During the first hour or two at that house, I became aware that there was a certain buzz in the room that I couldn't quite put my finger on. Apart from my tiny foray into the world of cannabis a couple of years previously with Jim Morrison, I still had little experience or knowledge of drugs but now looking back I am fairly sure that some of the party members were indulging in a particular illegal activity involving the use of the nasal passages and I am fairly sure that I was invited to join in – but not knowing what I was being invited to join in with, I said no, I'd stick to the alcohol.

It was well past lunchtime and I was wondering if I should be making a move to leave, when Andy told me he was going to go and have a lie down because he felt tired and had a busy night ahead. No way was this an invitation to join him. He wasn't making a pass, he was going to pass out. At least I think that's the way it was.

I felt kind of relieved about this – I didn't want to sleep with him anyway, partly because of The Boss, partly because, although I felt that I should fancy him like crazy, I didn't actually want to have sex with him, and partly because I knew I should be heading home. I didn't want to have to fib about where I'd been. So when Andy said he was going for a lie down, I said I would just go to the bathroom then I would leave myself.

'Oh come and use my bathroom,' he offered. And so he led me into his room and to the loo that ran off it. In I went and spent a few minutes in there freshening up.

And when I came out, there was Andy Williams, lying flat out on the bed on his back, fast asleep, snoring very softly. He was in that special kind of a deep, dreamless sleep.

I gingerly sat down on the edge of his bed and looked at him. I took in his high forehead, his hair, his mouth, half smiling even in his sleep, his eyelids, his strong jaw, his tanned good-quality skin with the wrinkles beginning to show. I took in all of it, trying to fix this very private view of my Last Teen Hero in my memory forever. Then I bent over and kissed his forehead and whispered, 'Bye, Andy. Thanks.' And I crept out of the room and left his house and his life.

Was it a let down? Did I not want to be seduced? No I didn't. I think originally that may have been his intention, but things changed, and no it wasn't a let down. I just wanted my own close up, my own moment. And I got that just fine without the embarrassment of having to say 'no'. It was a shame that he didn't know I had thanked him, nor what I was thanking him for – but apart from that, it was perfect.

Whether or not I had been with The Boss, and even if Andy Williams and I had ended up in bed together, we wouldn't have had more than a fleeting relationship, a one-nighter. I liked him, I found him polite, warm and gentle – and he had fabulously holdable hands. But really, we didn't have a lot in common and I am sure he found me too quiet, too silly and, in a funny way, too old fashioned, to be anything more than a day's interest in his life.

Next day in my handbag, I found the IOU note he had written me in return for me giving him my cigarette lighter. I can't remember why he wanted the lighter, I don't recall him smoking, but perhaps he did, or perhaps it was for someone else. I still have that note today. I never got the lighter back but who cares? The note's much better.

Early in August I received an invitation to go to the Park Suite at the Dorchester for a reception for a new West End show – *Jesus Christ Superstar*. The show was already causing controversy because of its subject matter. It had opened in New York in 1971 and made a star of Yvonne Elliman, who I had trekked all the way out to Great Yarmouth to see at the behest of impresario Robert Stigwood some time earlier. I'd found her pure of voice but a trifle boring.

The West End production was to open at the Palace Theatre and the lunchtime reception was packed out and I could hardly get in the door. Standing in the melee near the entrance, looking like an apologetic teenage virgin but somehow still managing to make himself noticable for that very reason, was a small guy with longish dark hair and vestages of hippydom about him, as if he had once played an acoustic guitar around a fire at every summer festival, but had now been told to smarten up and grow up by his dad. He had a worried air, his face was almost contorted with what could have been the effort of smiling at people when really he wanted to run away. He was obviously forcing himself to greet anyone who entered. I immediately felt deeply sorry for him.

He grabbed my hand and pumped it over-enthusiastically.

'Thank you for coming! Good to see you! I'm Andrew Lloyd Webber. Have a drink …' he waved in the direction of the other side of the room where Tim Rice was holding forth near the bar in a much more relaxed way.

They were both very young, of course. Within weeks the pair had a mammoth West End hit and I never had cause to feel sorry for Lloyd Webber again. Later I went to see the show, with Paul Nicholas as Jesus and Dana Gillespie as Mary. Yes, I enjoyed it, yes it was good in the manner of several

shows of that era – *Hair, Godspell* and so on. It was theatre
for pop music fans, and there was nothing wrong with that.
Later the duo were to make a star of another of my old
acquaintances – Elaine Paige.

Back at the office in Southampton Street, the old staff were
slowly being replaced by others. Betty was still Ed, Bev was
the new picture editor whose boyfriend Martyn took a lot
of the photos. Tom, whose real name was Brian, was the art
editor, John Fearn, the old art then Ass Ed, had been killed in
a car crash and Fid was now in his place. Sue James was the
new fashion editor who right from the moment she arrived
had the confidence, demeanour and aplomb of a future
senior manager, and soon became Betty's close ally.

While I was never going to be management or editor
material like Sue obviously was, Betty had by now realised
that I could be trusted on most levels to represent the
mag and her in a proper manner. More than anything, she
perceived that I was good with the readers and so I would
often be the one to do the 'Dream Come Trues' – the early,
original and best version of *Jim'll Fix It*. Every week in the
'mag' there was a form for the readers to fill in, saying what
their dream was. And every couple of weeks, we would select
one and make their dream come true. I enjoyed this as I could
select the dreams that I also would enjoy doing and having
spent the past few years seeing most of my own teenage
dreams come true, it seemed appropriate.

And it was fun (like being the judge at the disco dancing
thing) to play god with the teenybopper's hopes and prayers
and to feel benevolent and superior all at once when you

watched them achieve their dream, thanks to you and your Solomon powers.

For some strange reason, an early Dream Come True in September involved me arriving with two tiny teenage girls at the Hawaiian-themed restaurant at the top of the modern hotel, the Inn on the Park, Park Lane, to meet up with Betty Hale and a guy who had got lucky with a few hit records and a way with creating manufactured pop – Jonathan King.

The evening was a disaster – the little girls hardly spoke and neither did Jonathan King – at least not to them. While he chatted away to Betty, presumably because he felt she might be useful to him, he more or less ignored the girls and I found him rude, arrogant and boring. No doubt, if my readers had been two teenage boys he would have had a whole different take on the evening.

Shortly after that I had my first holiday with The Boss – we flew to Tunisia for two weeks during which time I got severe sunburn of the knees and chronic food poisoning from the alarming red Tunisian sausages which we were served for breakfast, lunch and dinner every day.

I also nearly drowned in the deceptively vicious sea off Hammamet due to the fact that I couldn't swim properly but had too much pride to inform The Boss, a veritable fish brought up by the Kent coast, of this. I was rescued, as The Boss swam, unconcerned about my shouting (presumably – hopefully – he thought I was just yelling in a having fun kind of way).

The person who rescued me was a weedy little guy, even thinner than me, even paler than me and with long red hair, just like me. After the third time I came up from the deep, screaming, by this time quite loudly, he plucked me up in his arms and somehow got me back to the shore where he lay me down and helped me cough up the lake of seawater I'd swallowed. The Boss eventually sauntered over, 'What's the matter with you,' he grinned. 'The waves aren't very tall!'

By this time my rescuer was also lying on the sand, exhausted due to the effort of carrying someone who definitely weighed more than he did out of the waves. The Boss just gave him a filthy look and walked back into the swell.

Back in London it was a fairly boring October during which period I interviewed Rick Springfield (anyone remember him?), Peter Skellern (Lieutenant Pidgeon), Chairmen of the Board, Steve Ellis of Love Affair, Colin Bluntstone and, for the umpteenth time, Johnny ('I Can See Clearly Now') Nash, who always asked me out every time I saw him and who, always, I declined not because he wasn't fabulous looking or because I didn't fancy him, which I did, in a mildish kind of way, but because of The Boss.

By this time, things were beginning to hot up in the UK for The Osmonds. Their appearance at the Royal Command Performance the previous May at the Palladium had started the fan fever which by autumn had turned into full blown Osmondmania with 14-year-old Donny the main object of teen affection – he'd been at number 1 throughout the summer with his single 'Puppy Love'.

But the other brothers were popular as well and the whole family were to arrive in the UK at the end of October to promote the new Osmond single, 'Crazy Horses'. The older brothers were hoping to sell themselves as not just another teenybop band but as great rockers, singers and musicians in their own right. However their stab at credibility was somewhat marred by the release in the same month of their small brother 'Little Jimmy' Osmond's novelty single, 'Long Haired Lover From Liverpool'.

'LHLFL' managed to get to number 1 and stayed at the top for several weeks during the Christmas holiday period, rather overshadowing The Osmonds' three weeks at number 2 for 'Crazy Horses'.

Over the past few months I had spoken to one or other of The Osmonds on the phone to do interviews for *Fab* with increasing regularity, and by the time of their visit I felt I knew most of them rather well, including their mother, Olive, and father, George, both of whom took an extremely keen interest in the boys' careers and were, basically, their managers, minders, PRs, promotion experts and PAs all rolled into one.

I had begun to realise that The Osmonds were a strong team, highly professional, and quite determined to grab every opportunity – as long as it didn't conflict with their strong Mormon beliefs which included no alcohol, drugs or tobacco, no caffeine, a healthy diet, no swearing. Not exactly rock world compatible, but there you are. Many years later, The Killers found huge success and they were Mormon too.

On the afternoon of Tuesday 31 October, then, I headed to the Churchill Hotel to meet ... The Jackson Five who, by coincidence, were also in the UK doing promotion at the same time, staying at the same hotel as Donny and co.

As I got near, I could hear screaming and shouting through the closed taxi windows, and as we turned into Portman Square I was surprised to find a mass of teenage girls outside the main entrance and scurrying around up and down Seymour Street alongside. Most of the fans, judging by the banners, hats and apparel they wore, were waiting to glimpse The Osmonds rather than The Jacksons. Compared with the fanbase of just a few months earlier it was a definite improvement.

I got out of the taxi, headed up into the entrance and found myself being pushed, prodded and shouted at by the nearest of the fans.

I and some other music journalists spent a couple of hours with The Jacksons, who were, at the time in sales terms, much bigger than The Osmonds in the UK after a string of hits including 'I Want You Back', 'I'll be There', and 'ABC'. Of the five, it was Michael – tiny, shy, with a complete halo of curly black hair surrounding his beautiful face – who most captivated me. He was just 14 years old but looked much younger and was happiest when talking about his friendship with Donny Osmond, his older friend at nearly 15. For all one read about the huge rivalry between the two bands and the two young lead singers, in fact they were good friends. Donny and Michael shared so much in terms of similar backgrounds, you could see why they liked to swap notes.

And two days later I was back at The Churchill to see The Osmonds themselves. I made my way up to room 516 and, with the history of phone calls behind us, we got on rather well. I did a taped interview with Donny and then talked to all the boys, as well as Mother and Father. The Osmonds never called their parents mum and dad, or ma and pa – it had to be Mother and Father, as decreed by Father George Osmond.

Not for the last time, I began trying to find chinks in the stock Osmond armour of big smiles, helpful answers, a permanent positive take on their lives, and a humble attitude to success, fans, their career and so on. And, not for the last time, I found that a hard one to crack. There was nothing bad or negative about them that I could write on the strength of this meeting, unless I were to resort to sarcasm about their teen following or their lack of street cred – something I wasn't about to do. Especially as the term street cred hadn't been invented then.

As we were all told years later in various articles and autobiographies, the Osmond life was, of course, far from perfect and indeed their demeanour was in part a smokescreen at least some of the time. It turned out later that Father Osmond had been a hard taskmaster during these early years – not averse to giving the boys a thump if they didn't do as told. Not being an Osmond Brother didn't seem like an option to any of them at the time. But because I didn't have to pretend to be intellectual and because they seemed very happy with the 'what's your favourite colour?' line of questioning ('Purple!') in truth I found them quite relaxing to be around that afternoon. The only stress-inducer was remembering not to swear and having to go without a cigarette. They wouldn't have objected, I found out later, but it only seemed polite.

Some sell-out gigs around London followed and by this time The Osmonds had begun making the pages of the national newspapers because of their ability to cause riots. One evening I journeyed up to the Rainbow Theatre in Finsbury Park to see them perform for the first time. The hysteria and screaming put even my Beatles '60s Albert Hall concert in the shade. And the boys performed a better set than I had anticipated, from what little I could hear.

By the time The Osmonds had departed they had definitely arrived, and in the weeks that followed Betty Hale and Olive Osmond began discussing a joint project which was, in 1973, to become *Osmonds' World* magazine – a monthly publication which would appear to be The Osmonds' own magazine, but which would be published by IPC, edited by Betty, and in part written – ghosted – by me.

The few weeks to the end of the year were busy with all kinds of interviews – by this time I was moonlighting for several other publications, including *Easy Listening* magazine and *Record Mirror*, to earn a little more money. This also had the benefit of broadening my field of work a bit – but still not in the direction of my one-time colleague Julie Webb. I was never going to be a *NME* or *Sounds* 'proper' music journalist. For *Easy Listening* I interviewed Jackie Trent and Tony Hatch – famous at the time as 'Mr and Mrs Music' – down at their Kent house, and Sacha Distel.

The Distel interview – backstage at the Prince of Wales theatre during a long season he did there with a few guests stars including Olivia Newton-John – was interesting for one thing that happened during the interview. The dressing room was quite cramped and somehow I ended up squashed behind the door, while he sat in the only other chair at the other side of the room directly in front of the door. He was being his usual charming Gallic flirty self, chatting about his family life and what a good guy he was and how his wife trusted him. I was getting quite bored. Then, towards the end of the interview, the door suddenly swung open, hiding me behind it, and as it did so a young female voice exclaimed, 'Oh, Sacha darling, I've missed you …' and I watched as this slim young female strode across the room, all blonde hair, lithe limbs and expensive clothes, and kissed Sacha passionately on the lips. Wondering why his response was less than enthusiastic and, no doubt, why he was beginning to blush, she looked round and saw me sitting there.

Then she, too, began to blush – 'Oh, oh … sorry, I was just … I'll catch up with you later, Sacha …' she tailed off, and legged it out again.

And thus I was left wondering if there was more to the working relationship between Sacha Distel and Olivia Newton-John than most people realised.

eight

That's Neat, That's Neat, That's Neat

1973

The hippy/flower power/protest era is dead – we're all bored with watching Joan Baez and Dylan drone on and we want a lot more fun. So glam rock and bubblegum are here and suddenly the charts are full with simple songs from The Sweet, Glitter and co. that make you smile and get up and dance. *Top of the Pops* is awash with silver platforms, long hair and too much make up, and that's only the boys. We're watching *Some Mothers Do 'Ave Em, Are You Being Served?* and, to add a bit of culture (but only a bit) we have the movie version of *Jesus Christ Superstar*.

Of course I loved most of the bubblegum and glam rock – it was around my level of musical intellect. The biggest successes of the year were artistes created by the indies and newer managements companies and labels such as Dick Leahy and Bell, with Gary Glitter, and Mickie Most with his RAK Records and music publishing. With writers Nicky Chinn and Mike Chapman he made huge stars of Suzi Quatro and Sweet – and turned a four-piece band who had been batting away for several years trying to make it into the charts, into one of the biggest pop groups of 1973–75. Their name was Mud. By the later years of the decade, this was, literally, true, but for a few years they had hit after hit and became one of my favourite groups of young men – because they were just so damn nice to be around.

I first met the Mud boys – Les Gray, Dave Mount, Ray Stiles and Rob Davis – up at Tony Barrow International PR. Barrow had done The Beatles' publicity for several years in the '60s then struck out on his own, and in the '70s became possibly the most successful music PR in London. He was a pleasant man who had wonderful parties for the artistes he represented, including Cilla Black, The Jacksons, and very many others.

A good PR was worth almost more than anything to the bands of this era – they could get all the journos along to do interviews with the most dire people by a mix of charm, flattery, wheedling, cajoling, and blackmail in the best possible manner (you come and interview this band now and later, when I have someone really hot, you can get an exclusive …). While most of Barrow's artistes weren't particularly dire, Mud didn't have a great deal going for them at the time after several years of single flops and no great image to recommend them. Even after they were taken on board by RAK and Chinn/Chapman in late 1972, things were slow to change for the four men from Mitcham, Surrey. Although the first two singles released in 1973 crept into the charts, it wasn't until the autumn that 'Dyna-mite' stayed in the top 10 for five weeks and, finally, Mud was flying.

They were perfect *Fab 208* material as the tunes were happy, basic, beaty things, the boys were clean-cut, brother-types, and they were a good live band, better than they were given credit for. They could also hardly believe that their luck was changing at last, and thus were anxious, almost over-anxious, to do every single bit of promotion that was put their way, including almost endless interviews with me, or, I am sure, so it must have seemed to them.

They'd travel miles to do things like *Fab* readers' parties, which were held several times a year in all corners of the country, and would never turn a photo opportunity down. After a while it became apparent, according to Georgina, who for some reason occasionally accompanied me on these forays, that the drummer, Dave Mount, had taken a fancy to me.

It became apparent to me, too, when Les Gray sidled up to me one day and asked if I'd go out for a drink with Dave. Now Dave was a lovely boy – not the best looking of the team, but nevertheless the kind of guy you could trust with your life. But of course, being with The Boss, I wasn't available. Truly, if Dave had been Andy Williams I would have gone for a drink with him, but he wasn't, so it wasn't worth giving him hope when I knew I just wasn't ever going to fancy him. So I said no.

Shortly afterwards, we all headed up North for a readers' party (I believe it was Leeds but it could have been Glasgow or Newcastle – going to these parties was like being an American tourist in Europe; you never quite knew where you were) and I had the problem of getting all the Mud news and angles and quotes about the party, the town, and so on, while doing my best to make sure that Dave didn't think I was leading him on, and also doing my best to make sure that he was kept happy and sweet. This was why falling for and/or going out with the people one was paid to interview wasn't a particularly good idea, I was beginning to realise.

It was in April that, thanks to The Osmonds, I finally got on a plane and headed out to The States.

I hate sharing the bedroom with Veronica Hill – and I know she hates sharing with me. She won't let me have Luxy on under the bedclothes at night and she does spiteful things to try to keep me awake, like pinching my feet. Thank God she's gone away for now – she got herself a job with horses, down in the West Country, so I have the bedroom to myself. I have my poster of Richard Chamberlain on the wall and next to that, I have another poster – an aerial shot of Los Angeles, showing the dual-carriageways snaking across the city, the cadillacs and the skyscrapers of downtown … I often stare at that poster taking in every little detail as much as I take in Dr Kildare's blue eyes and the rest of his face.

One day, I am going to go there. It's got to be the most exciting place on earth. Imagine – living in the city where all the movies are made, where the TV shows are made. Where you might bump into people you see on the screen, just walking around, just shopping, in the bars …

In my early teens, I truly thought that Los Angeles was the holy grail. Even at 15 to go there was my main ambition. I recently found an old school essay book and in it, an essay we'd been asked to write titled 'Castles in the Air'. The only teacher I liked at Bicester Grammar School was the English teacher, whose name, sadly, I can't recall. He had had polio so his body was in a pretty poor state, but he was a wonderful man, the kind of teacher schools should hope and pray they find, because he was encouraging, patient, and with a wicked humour. I loved him, actually – he saved my school life, he really did, as well as giving me the confidence to believe that one day I really might be able to write for a living. So I put all my energies into giving him essays he could enjoy. Extract from 'Castles in the Air':

I for one, hope to have many years before me in which, after dreaming, I can attempt to make each dream come true. Most ambitions are possible … to take a defeatist attitude from the start is to squash any hope of fulfilling them.

After analysing each one of my secret hopes, I find that they are all possible. For instance, I want to visit the USA more than anything else. I also want to work in Fleet Street, write books, and meet a well-known person who shall remain anonymous [this was Billy Fury but I was too embarrassed to say so in this essay, prompting the teacher to write 'spoilsport' in the margin].

Many people work in Fleet Street, so why not me? Then I could go to America, to work as a correspondent, for example, and write books as a side interest. From such a position, I would meet many famous people.

I know that most of us dream of wealth and happiness. Happiness I would gain from my work, and I never want to be overloaded with money in any case [that was a good job, then]. This all sounds very boastful now, but even if it is only wishful thinking, in about fifty years' time I will be able to look back with some amusement at my young ambitions…'.

'Some amusement' is a bit of an understatement; the earnest and pompous way I wrote was hilarious. But every bit of it came true – even down to looking back on the predictions years later. Thank God for castles in the air, I say.

The States trip, which was planned for 14 to 21 April, was for two main reasons. Firstly, it was to see The Osmonds in their own country, performing, and to spend enough time with them all to enable me to begin writing articles for the forthcoming *Osmonds' World* magazine, which I was to spend the next few years compiling virtually single-handed (with Osmond help, of course).

Secondly, it was the prize trip of a lifetime for a young girl who had applied, via Dream Come True in *Fab*, to meet Donny Osmond.

When we had announced the competition, we had received thousands of entries (at that time, what teenage girl didn't want to meet Donny Osmond?). After sifting through and coming up with a shortlist of ten or so likely candidates for the trip, I talked to them on the phone or visited them in person to find the ideal reader to take to America to meet Donny. This wasn't the normal way competitions worked, but it was a 'dream come true' rather than an actual competition, so we could make the rules up as we went along – and the last thing I wanted to do was take with me a reader who wouldn't enjoy the trip, who would find it daunting, who would get to meet Donny and then not say a word to him – you know the sort of thing. I had had enough experience by this time of wanting to strangle readers who, when faced with their idol, would just stand there and look dumb. (Anyone seen the photo of me at 16 with my idol Billy Fury, just standing there and looking dumb?)

I also wanted someone with whom I could rub along for the duration. Judi Matthews, who was around 14 at the time, turned out to fit the bill as well as anyone and thus on 14 April, The Boss kindly drove us to Heathrow for our Trans World Airlines (TWA) flight to LA.

Having spent nearly six years working for *Fab*, having been abroad several times and having met everyone on my wish list, it took quite a lot to get me excited, but I remember so well, thinking, at last, I am going to the States. I am going to LA!

The fact that I wasn't having to pay a penny for the trip, that I was getting paid to go, and that I was going to be seeing a sheaf of stars while out there was all rather good.

We were met at LA airport by Cyril Maitland, *Fab*'s long-serving photographer out there. Cyril was a short, bearded man probably in his 40s, who obviously knew LA inside out. We arrived at our hotel, The Roosevelt in Hollywood, and in my spacious room there was a big bowl of fruit and a note saying, 'Welcome to LA – love from The Osmonds'. Nice.

During three hectic days in Hollywood and LA, Cyril took us to Disneyland, to the beach, to various authentic American diners, to meet Ben Murphy (who was the star of a huge '70s TV series called *Alias Smith and Jones*) at his condominium block apartment, to meet Mark Spitz, the swimmer who had just won a chestful of golds at the 1972 Olympics, and to the American equivalent magazine of *Fab* which was called *Sixteen*.

On Wednesday 18th we took the short flight to Las Vegas and checked into the Tropicana Hotel, where we stayed for two days and met up with Betty Hale, who had flown out from the UK. She'd arrived on the pretext of having a business meeting with the Osmond parents re. *Osmonds' World*, but I have the feeling she may have felt the need to check up on how I was coping with everything – looking after Judi, doing interviews, finding my way around, and so on. I think the verdict was favourable, which was no surprise – I was more or less grown up.

It was in Vegas, at Caesars Palace, that Judi finally got to meet Donny Osmond before the show, and had a front of house seat for The Osmonds' performance, during which Donny sang to her. It was during this short run that Marie Osmond was finally given her chance to take to the stage – she sang a duet with Donny and although she was nervous she got through it okay. She was wearing a long gown, with full heavy make-up and an old-fashioned hairdo, and I remember wondering if the whole look was such a good idea. Within weeks she was topping the charts in the USA and UK with her first single, 'Paper Roses'.

One of my tasks on *Osmonds' World* magazine was to write the Marie Osmond problem page, a feat that took some dexterity of thought and pen, as Marie was a 13-year-old virgin; had never dated a boy – in fact, had hardly even seen any boys apart from her brothers, as far as I could tell – and wasn't going to be allowed to date until she was 16 in any case; had never been to school (all the Osmonds were taught by correspondence courses in between gigs) and had a mindset as far removed from the average UK teenager as you could imagine. But I got by.

Next day we drove with the Osmonds up to Lake Tahoe, a leisure and gaming resort near San Francisco, where the family rented a lakeside villa. It was at this villa that Olive Osmond suddenly produced for me a paperback copy of

The Book of Mormon, and, after reading a few passages from it for me, proceeded to round up as many members of the family as she could to sign it. She managed to get all the signatures except for Jimmy, who had disappeared down to the lake to get up to some boyhood mischief. I wasn't sure if it was an unsubtle hint that I should read the book (they can't have failed to notice by this time that I drank alcohol and caffeine and smoked tobacco and was in definite need of saving) or simply a nice gesture from Mrs Osmond with no strings attached. I took it as the latter. And spent a while wondering how they reconciled their religion with the gambling, drinking, fast-living town of Las Vegas that they chose to perform in so often.

After a couple of hours chatting to the family and gazing out at the expanse of ice-blue water, which reminded me, in its boring beauty, of the lakes of Sweden, Judi and I headed by taxi down the coast a few miles to the Sahara resort where we were staying, and watched The Osmonds perform there in the evening. Finally, on the Saturday we flew back to LA and caught the flight home. Judi had been a real trouper, she'd enjoyed herself and we had had no arguments, and although the trip had been too crammed to actually take much of it in properly, for me it was a taster.

Once home I realised that, in fact, I would *not* like to live in LA, my initial impression being that it was a rather one-horse town of little charm; I would *not* like to spend much time in a resort like Vegas or Tahoe – where every time I touched the elevator buttons I got an electric shock, that's how wired the places were. Little Jimmy Osmond's hair literally stood on end as he got out of the lift at the Tahoe Sahara to walk through the side of the casino area, which, luckily, he found hugely funny, but I was annoyed that my camera wasn't to hand.

As soon as I got back to London from the States, The Boss and I flew to Portugal for a late spring holiday, and when we returned I received two press tickets for the forthcoming David Bowie concert at Earls Court on 12 May. On the day, we walked from Avonmore Road down the Warwick Road to the Earls Court Exhibition Centre and as we approached we began to see dozens and dozens of fans, male and female, all dressed in slightly different versions of Ziggy Stardust.

We sat feeling rather old and boring, as Ziggy acted and sang and played on stage in front of 10,000 crazy, shouting, dancing fans. It wasn't my favourite music, he wasn't one of my favourite performers either – but I had to admit, he had brought himself a long way since the day I first saw him up at *Fab*.

A few weeks later, I saw another very popular David – the latest star of pop and the West End stage, David Essex. Like Bowie, Mud and several others, he had spent several years trying to find elusive chart success but had finally 'cracked it' when he won the lead role in the musical *Godspell* which had been a sell-out at Wyndham's Theatre since November 1971. He was also the star of the pop culture movie *That'll be the Day* – a story about a fairground worker who becomes a pop star – which also starred my old friends Keith Moon and Billy Fury, and had been released just a few weeks before our meeting.

I met him, and his long-term manager, Derek Bowman, backstage before his performance and David, bless him, was trying as hard as hard could be to be laid back about his sudden huge success both in the movie and stage worlds. He bounded into the dressing room like a lanky puppy and began his role of the afternoon – to charm me and impress upon me how natural and ordinary and East End he was.

I sat there taping his replies but was too transfixed by his lower legs to pay any real attention to what he was saying at the time. The expanse of skinny, hairy, ghostly pale-fleshed ankle exposed below half-mast trousers, the white socks, the huge black shoes which almost filled my line of view as he sat, legs crossed, in front of me, held a strange and bewitching fascination. Legs and feet that were a complete turn off on the hot sex symbol of the day. It was so weird. I found, when I could tear myself away from his lower regions, that he did have a beautiful face with these huge blue sad gypsy come-to-bed eyes. They were a close second to Nimoy for twinkle rating, too, when he smiled – but they didn't do a thing for me because, unlike Nimoy, all his twinkling and all the rest of it just didn't seem sincere. Probably mean of me, but that's the way I felt. And you know by now what a good judge of men I've always been.

Forgive me, David, I am sure your legs are just lovely now. I don't think you'd grown into your looks at that time, you were just too young.

A few weeks later I came back to the same place to see the same person, but this time with a reader, Karen Gill, for a Dream Come True meet and greet. To be fair, Essex was very pleasant to, and patient with, the young fan and it was a date she remembered for decades – a fact I know because she was still writing to me talking about it well into the '90s.

Around the same time, I interviewed Chris Jagger, in my opinion the nicer of the two Jagger brothers, who was trying to make it as an actor, and I also had the chance to observe Bianca Jagger up close, at a reception at The Ritz. She strode in as if she owned the place, beautifully turned out in a very sharp black trouser suit, with short, perfectly groomed black hair, and holding a walking cane (for show, not use) with a gold handle. There were also two gay men trailing in her wake. She shook hands with two other men, and they all sat down at a table about 5ft from me. The talk was obviously business and I wasn't interested in the subject – but what fascinated me was her self-confidence, her attitude and her manner. She was sharper than her suit and dominated her companions throughout. I realised that she must wear the trousers at home as well.

The Boss had his own busy social and business life but, because his office was just a few doors from mine, in Maiden Lane, right next to Rules restaurant for whom he worked as the PR, we often saw each other at lunchtime and would also meet in Rules after work. Sometimes I'd take him to one of my freebie bashes – in June, for instance, we sat and yawned our way through *Applause* at the Haymarket Theatre, starring Lauren Bacall. Miss Bacall was one of the last of the great Hollywood stars, but in our opinion, her stage acting career was something she should have reconsidered.

Later in the year, we went to one of the best parties ever – a bash at The Dorchester held by Bell records for Gary Glitter in recognition of all the records he had sold. The bit that sticks in my mind is Alan 'Fluff' Freeman, the disc jockey, wearing some kind of female fancy dress and sitting on a 'throne' near the stage area, surrounded by young, handsome male fairies dressed all in white robes. Freeman was the guest of honour because, so the story went, he was largely responsible for the Glitter phenomenon because he was the only DJ who had spotted the potential of the first hit, 'Rock and Roll Parts 1 and 2', and played it non-stop on his Radio 1 show. Freeman thus had a lot to answer for.

The Boss remembers going to the (male) loo and finding Suzi Quatro in there, shouting and kicking a locked door 'Come on, Len, what the fuck are you doing ….'. Len Tuckey was her guitarist, and her husband, but they divorced a while later. The place was actually heaving with all the stars of the day, you'd tread on them every time you moved – so much so that when we got home it was a great relief to sit down with a cup of tea and watch TV. Z Cars or Z-list stars? Take your choice. Maybe I was suffering the beginnings of disillusion with the whole pop scene. You can have too much of a good thing.

In return for these freebies and fun, The Boss would treat me to unlimited drinks in the bar of Rules. Rules restaurant was supposed to be a bastion of fine and discreet English dining. 'London's oldest restaurant' according to the PR blurb that was always handed out (this claim, still bandied about today, was totally invented, I have to say, by The Boss).

However, the barman, Buck, ran his little bar area just inside the main entrance as an independent state. If you were prepared to pay his prices, you could just pop in for a drink like it was your local pub without having to have a meal. Plenty of people – including the stars from nearby West End shows at The Savoy, the Vaudeville and the Adelphi, most of the staff of *Woman's Own* magazine from Southampton Street round the corner, an assortment of Fleet Street photographers, hacks and cartoonists, including Jak of the *Evening Standard* and Frank Dickens, spent more hours than any of them would care to recall at 'Buck's bar', as it was always known. Whoever was there, Buck would introduce you; it was his own daily cocktail party.

Buck was a superbly entertaining barman as well as a good-hearted man, a shoulder to cry on at times, and at others, a wily guy who had every trick in the book for making a few extra pennies out of his little empire and for keeping you there as long as possible – not that anyone ever complained. Sometimes he would get out a game called *Shut the Box*, or he'd start a game of spoof, and it was fun to sit on the bar stools and just see what would happen next.

What happened one time was that a female snake charmer arrived, hot from one of the local shows, clutching a case which, indeed, contained a python. The Boss, having had a few drinks by this time, persuaded her it would be fun to let the snake out. She did and off it slithered amongst the tables and diners. The mayhem that followed within seconds was wonderful, and the incident made the *Evening Standard*.

Whether this gave The Boss, who was being paid plenty to do Rules' public relations (in an ironic sort of way, obviously), brownie points or not, I am not sure. The owner at the time, John Wood, veered between being delighted that he made so much money out of the bar, and being annoyed that his straight-laced restaurant seemed at times more like the rowdiest boozer or wildest circus in town.

Another time I caused the stir. The tables in the bar area were laid with large thick linen tablecloths, and that day The Boss, a couple of people from *Woman's Own* and I had ordered a large jug of buck's fizz and four champagne glasses. They all arrived, and suddenly one of the *WO* people remembered that old trick, where you pull the cloth off the table and leave everything else in place.

'Which one of you is going to attempt this feat?' she said.

'Oh, that'll be easy – I'll do it!' I replied. And before The Boss could stop me, One … Two … Three … I counted, gripped the edge of the tablecloth and pulled, as hard and as fast as I could, with my eyes shut. When I opened them – the champagne, the glasses, everything, were still on the table.

'There! No problem …'. I said, nonchalantly. That story had a long run.

It was in this tiny bar that I bumped into Liza Goddard again, and it was here that I met Joe Brown and his wife Vicky, Jean Simmonds the film actress, Millicent Martin, Anna Massey and Max Wall, the music hall comedian who was plotting his career revival in a new stage version of *The Entertainer*. The Boss and I would often have lunch with him and listen while Max monologued in that distinctive voice about his miserable life, his dreadful marriage and anything else on his mind. Eventually, once I had got over the slight thrill of lunching with a legend, I came to dread Max arriving unnannouced at our table and asking if we'd mind if he joined us – he was a nice guy, I guess, no harm in him, but boy, he was self-centred. Max did always seem depressed – like so many of the great comics.

It was also in Buck's bar that we met our American friends Wyn and Gerry. They collected celebrities like other people collect discount vouchers, and it didn't take them long to cotton on to the potential of Rules. One day they invited us to their Belgravia mews house for Sunday lunch, with a promise of a 'real great entertainer' on the guest list. He turned out to be the comedian Frankie Howerd. Frankie arrived on his own, his latest boyfriend having let him down, and for the first fifteen minutes was very jolly, his TV self, full of 'oohs' and 'aaahs' and high-pitched squeals and raised eyebrows. But suddenly, and over the course of thirty seconds flat, he did a 100 per cent personality switch, and for the next two hours was so morose that at one point we thought of putting him on suicide watch.

In September The Boss and I finally got the energy to find ourselves a one-bedroom ground-floor flat with a garden in Cathcart Road, on the Chelsea/Fulham borders just off the Fulham Road. This was a giant step-up for me. I was getting further and further along the District line with each move towards the West End – now our nearest tube was South Kensington and we'd walk up there most days to catch the train to Embankment and then walk down The Strand to work.

I still hadn't begun to take for granted the pleasure of living and working among all the landmark streets and buildings of London. And we now had some famous neighbours. Our garden backed on to a larger garden in the posher Tregunter Road, and if we happened to be outside during the daytime or early evening, there would very often be the most amazing, booming, female voice carrying over the garden wall, shouting at her children. It didn't take us long to realise that the voice belonged to the *Avengers* actress, Honor Blackman. Even inside the flat, you could still here her booming on, and I got to feel quite sorry for her kids and the state of their ears.

Valerie Singleton from *Blue Peter* shopped at the little deli across in Hollywood Road, while popular young actress Judy Geeson was often in the queue at the greengrocery. Judy would shop carrying a small fluffy dog – she was way ahead of her time. Patrick Mower (Tom Haggerty of TV's *Special Branch*) would scream around the roads in an open-top sports car, looking as if he was quite fond of himself. And Leonard Rossiter, who became huge in 1974 with *Rising Damp*, would wander up and down the Fulham Road carrying his shopping in tatty old plastic bags, shooting slightly poisonous looks at anyone who dared to look at him first, which included me, once, but only the once.

After we came back from a holiday to Cyprus in the autumn, I went up to Notting Hill to interview one of the most popular TV stars at the time – Richard Beckinsale.

Richard later worked with Rossiter in *Rising Damp* and became better known as the star of *Porridge*, along with Ronnie Barker, but at this time he was famous for a TV sitcom called *The Lovers*, in which he had starred with Paula Wilcox.

The pilot episode of *Porridge* had been screened and Richard was waiting to discover if it would be turned into a series. I suppose some PR seemed in order for him, and so I arrived at his basement flat in a street off Notting Hill Gate.

As a celeb interviewer you're never quite sure what you're going to get. Sometimes people are as you think they will be, but often, they are not. And, as with any first meeting, some people you get on with better than others. With some interviews, you just both muddle along and hope that when your half hour or hour is up you'll have enough material to make a decent read, with others, you sit and listen and don't have to say a word, which sounds good, but often it means that you can't get a word in, to take the chat in a direction you want it to go. Some celebs who want the publicity but don't want to talk about their private lives will, quite deliberately, seize on a neutral topic and then manage to hold forth about it without ceasing for the full duration of the interview. And there were – and still are – plenty of celebs who will only answer yes, or no, or just raise an eyebrow to any question, or keep saying, 'I'm only here to talk about the film/TV show/album.'

I was never the best interviewer in the world but I usually got by – and I did get better at unobtrusively directing the chat and getting what I wanted out of the celebs. Often, a shy, quiet and retiring manner would often get a better interview than any amount of hard-hitting, bullying tactics.

Richard Beckinsale was one of those people with whom I just clicked at first sight – we began chatting and giggling straight away, while he made us a cup of tea. After a few minutes I realised that he seemed to keep looking towards a door off the small sitting room.

'Is anything up?' I asked.

He looked a bit sheepish. 'Well, actually – I'm babysitting!' he said. 'We had a baby recently (he was with the actress Judy Loe, whom he later married). Would you like to see her?'

'Oh, yes please!'

I wasn't that comfortable with babies, having been the youngest, and the memory of trying to set Warren Carter on fire was still in my mind, but not to worry. Beckinsale virtually ran to the bedroom and, beaming from ear to ear with pride, brought out his daughter. While I held her, he went back for her cot. And so we spent the afternoon babysitting together, playing with the baby, who was beautiful and probably around 2 months old. I got well into the cooing and we had a great time swapping baby stories and horror babysitting stories, including the Warren incident which had Richard hooting with laughter.

I left Beckinsale, with what few celeb meetings ever gave you – a warm feeling in the pit of your stomach, like he was a really nice person, he wasn't just putting it on. How lucky Judy, and the little daughter, Kate, were to have such a lovely guy, I thought, for a husband and a dad. Within a few years he was dead from a heart attack, but the little girl grew up to do his memory proud. Thus I have babysat a huge Hollywood actress.

Around this time I decided I had to learn to drive. The nearest driving school was the BSM just off Trafalgar Square so I went along and signed up for a course of ten lessons. Having been driven around by The Boss for a couple of years, my impression of driving was that it was imperative to go everywhere as fast as the car would let you go, that it was imperative to shout and swear at all who got in your way, whether pedestrian or other driver, and that all women drivers were appalling and should never be allowed into the driving seat.

Although, then, my brain told me I should drive, my heart really wasn't in it. Quite frankly I was terrified. Thus it was that on my very first driving lesson I was dismayed to find, after ten minutes' chat, that I was expected to drive the vehicle down a road through Central London, albeit in second gear. We started to move and, to my horror, I saw a car coming towards us.

'Help!' I screamed. 'There's a car coming … what do I do?'

'Just stay on your side of the road and you'll be fine,' said the instructor patiently.

On my second lesson I found myself driving round Trafalgar Square. On another lesson, I was driving along the Euston Road in the inside lane and, glancing across to the middle lane, found myself staring straight at Jimmy Savile in his open-topped Roller. He waved his cigar at me and nearly had my bumper in his passenger door as he drove off. Whether he recognised me from *Top of the Pops* I wasn't sure. As he was at the height of his fame that was another moment I felt I really was right at the centre of the UK pop scene – as I said, I never was a good judge of people. But I did manage to pass my driving test first go.

The rest of the year included my first meeting with the charismatic Marc Bolan of T.Rex at the New Bond Street offices of Warrior Music. I was a huge fan of his music – every single was perfect pop, in my opinion – and he was quite beautiful to look at, in those days.

The next time I saw him, three years later when his popularity was diving and the hits had dried up, he arrived at a press reception near Tottenham Court Road for Dennis Waterman, who made a couple of records for the DJM label on the back of his success in The Sweeney. Why Bolan came to this event, I'm not sure, but I was shocked to see him. Overweight, overbearing, his young fresh looks already beginning to fade, he spent the whole occasion looking round the room to see who was looking at him, and trying to muscle in to every press shot that he could. In his lifetime, he never had another hit.

I also spent another few days with The Osmonds, who returned to the UK at the end of October for concerts and TV appearances, staying at the Britannia Hotel. By this time they were absolutely huge in the UK, with a string of hits from The Osmonds and Donny all year, and Marie about to release 'Paper Roses' in the UK. I went to Heathrow to meet them with photographer David Porter and we watched amazed as thousands of girls screamed and yelled and tried to get near the boys. I later found out that a viewing balcony had collapsed because of the amount of people on it – not even The Beatles in their heyday had received such adulation. Little Bill Sammeth had been right after all …

I was in constant contact with the family not only when they visited the UK, but by phone to Utah, because of *Fab* and because *Osmonds' World* magazine was a monthly sell-out. Olive had a great interest in the magazine and had her own column extolling the benefits of a close family and of having values in life.

As someone who smoked, drank, had had sex before marriage and generally did not live a particularly wholesome life, I constantly amazed myself at how well I interpreted the Osmond line and converted it into copy for the magazine. Everything went back to the States to be approved before going to press, and I don't recall the family ever wanting to change anything I had written. Perhaps deep down there was an Osmond clone inside me dying to get out …

Also in November, I went along to see Elton John at the Inn on the Park, who was having a press reception for his latest album, *Goodbye Yellow Brick Road*. As I had been fixated on David Essex's legs, so I was fixated on John's wrist, as it held what was undoubtedly the most expensive watch I had ever seen – more or less the size of Big Ben and completely encrusted with diamonds. The rest of him was, relatively speaking, understated, but that soon changed.

A couple of weeks on, in late November, I was peculiarly nervous as I headed towards Peter Gormley's Savile Row management offices to meet, for the first time, the King of UK pop, Cliff Richard. As a youngster I had never been a great fan of Cliff – I used to have regular and heated arguments on the school bus with a girl who was an avid Cliff fan, about the merits or otherwise of Cliff versus Billy Fury. Since The Beatles' days Cliff had struggled to maintain his place in pop, and had been lumbered with a goodie-goodie image via his religious beliefs and his super-clean appearance when all around him were going down the hippie, then glam rock, then punk roads.

Indeed, so uncool was he considered that earlier in the year he had gone for broke and had sung the UK's Eurovision Song Contest entry, 'Power to All Our Friends'. In a few years' time he was to find his way back with a string of much more credible songs such as 'Devil Woman' and 'We Don't Talk Anymore' – but at this time things must have been quiet enough that the interview with *Fab 208* was agreed.

As I waited for him to arrive, my nerves grew, and I still didn't know why as he would surely be a little Osmond-like, and I could get along with them just fine. Perhaps it was like waiting to be have an audience with the mother superior of a convent. But as I waited a little more and watched as people put out the first of the Christmas decorations in a display window opposite, I realised that they had just presented me with my angle. I would talk to Cliff about Christmas.

He gave me a great interview and at the finish I realised I was another convert – not to Christianity (I had never been back to church since being confirmed at the age of 12) but to Cliff. He really was ok.

Now believe me, I don't have, and never have had, a leg fetish – but a few days later I had occasion to be sitting in the back of another West End office, on a low sofa, opposite yet another pair of strange legs. These were incredibly skinny legs. It was 27 November so it was quite cold, but the legs were bare below a miniskirt. And the legs were covered in long, dark hairs. I sat in my groundhog moment wondering why their owner didn't either a) shave or wax them or b) cover them up in thick dark warm tights.

The owner of the hirsute limbs, and the owner's husband, were chattering away opposite me not realising that my mind was on hairy legs rather than the new Wings album they were here to promote – *Band on the Run*.

Yes, the leg owner was Linda McCartney, and the husband was Paul.

Further on up, Linda had done something strange with the hair on her head, too – think of Rod Stewart in the Faces circa 1970 – long at the sides but short and spikey just at the top – and you have it. The cockatiel mullet. Not a good look. She wasn't wearing any make-up either.

I don't have any idea what we talked about that day. I just remember taking in the completely non-babe way Linda was, and then looking at her hubbie, who was nice enough if a bit prickly, and realising he was no looker either (you could think that sort of thing back in those days). Then I got to thinking back to the Albert Hall when I was a teen, there with my dad and Margaret Fox, screaming at The Beatles. Here is one quarter of that phenomenon and he's got hooded eyes, thin lips, slightly thinning hair, bit of a paunch – what on earth did we all see in him? Ah well. Perhaps he could sing. Perhaps he could write songs. Perhaps he just got lucky. I don't know.

So by the end of autumn 1973 I was able to cross several members of pop royalty – queens, kings, whatever – from my 'must meet' list. Elton John, Cliff Richard, Paul McCartney – pretty good. On 4 December I had my first encounter with a band who were not yet in that league of pop royalty but were obviously hoping to get there, because their name was, indeed, Queen.

I only went along because Tony Brainsby had asked me to go, more or less as a favour. He said he had this group of guys who were very good but hadn't done as well with their first two singles as had been hoped. 'There'll be plenty of refreshment and it will be a laugh I promise you ...'.

So I arrived at his SW1 terrace office in the early afternoon and immediately felt as though I had stepped, just like my first moment in the *Fab* offices but with much less light, into an *Alice in Wonderland* on speed kind of situation. The house was quite gloomy – Tony's mood lighting, I guess, or the lightbulbs had all gone – and rich with tobacco-type odours and haze. Fantastic music was blasting around the house from top to toe – and as I stood near the top of the narrow first flight of stairs, a crew of boys – obviously, from the look of them, Queen themselves, bashed their way through the entrance door and we all stood on the stairs, shaking hands, hugging, kissing and, eventually, falling over. They may have come straight from the pub – I know I had.

Tony peered down to see what was going on, realised we had introduced ourselves after a fashion, and just left us to it.

The music turned out to be Queen's first album. They had released it back in the summer and the lead singer Freddie Mercury, whose OTT behaviour, I finally realised, accounted for at least 75 per cent of the chaos that happened that afternoon, sang along with each track as it came.

'Come on, Jude, come on – be my backing singer, go on…'.

So I did a few la la las until he got engrossed with his own performance, finally bowing and flourishing as each track came to an end. He put on quite a show and by the end of the afternoon when I staggered away I knew – and this time I wasn't wrong – that this band would be big no matter what bad start they had had. Freddie had such a beautiful voice and you just couldn't ignore him. At all.

nine

Judy Teen Grew Sick of the Scene

1974 AND 1975

Abba win Eurovision with 'Waterloo'. Pantomime song and pantomime outfits. Then Mike Batt has a hit with 'The Wombles of WImbledon'; 10-year-old Lena Zavaroni sings 'Ma, He's Making Eyes at Me'; John Denver bores us all to tears with 'Annie's Song' – we're not living through the best of times for great pop music.

In fact, January 1974 was pretty boring and depressing all round. We were in the middle of a national State of Emergency called by the Conservative government under Ted Heath, due to the ongoing miners' strikes over pay. All kinds of rules meant a three-day working week, and there was a general sense around the *Fab* office of the good times having come to an end.

The most exciting things I could dredge up, apart from ongoing Osmond phone calls, were interviews with Cozy Powell and Medicine Head, a lunchtime gig at the Talk of the Town for Lorna Luft, Judy Garland's daughter, and a press reception at the old Les Ambassadeurs club for Lulu. I'd bumped into Lulu several times over the years and had always found her pleasant and helpful. One time in particular, in the fairly early days, when I would get embarrassed at any slight thing that went wrong, I went to a press 'do' for the NSPCC just north of Oxford Street. Rather than catching a taxi, I went by tube and when I came up from Oxford Circus station, it was bucketing down and I had no brolly. I had no choice but to hurry to the gig, arriving absolutely drenched and with no semblance of dignity or style left.

As I stood at the entrance wondering whether to go in or not, Lulu, who must have been either a guest of honour or patron, or both, appeared from inside. When she saw this drowned rat, rather than turn her nose up and walk past, she immediately turned into a complete mother hen.

'Och, look at you – not to worry, we'll get you sorted out.'

'Rain wasn't forecast,' I said feebly.

She led me to the Ladies, opened her bag and produced tissues and whatever else she deemed necessary, and helped me to make myself presentable again. She then walked with me into the reception and introduced me to a few people. After that, I had lots of time for her. Although over the intervening thirty-odd years she seems to have got a bit more grand, I always remember how kind she was.

By March, as correctly predicted by me – for once – Queen at last had their first UK top 10 hit with 'Seven Seas of Rhye' and a hit album, *Queen II*. They were on their way.

And by March we had a new prime minister, Harold Wilson, back for his second term after a four-year break. After the most depressing winter I could ever remember, there was small cause for hope. Not that I ever was a fan of Wilson – shallow as I was, I just couldn't cope with his appearance, having never warmed to pipe-smoking, overweight, Gannex-mac-wearing men. Christ, the guy was only in his 50s at this time – younger than I am now – and he looked so old and out of touch with youth – the very people that the Labour party needed to win over.

I spent most of the summer getting Mud on my shoes all over the place because I was writing their life story for *Fab*. Once Dave Mount had realised I wasn't going to go out with him, he was fine about it and since our first few meetings in 1973, we had become good friends within the band/work context. When they finally had their first monster smash hit, 'Tiger Feet', early in 1974, I was delighted. Even after that, and as the hits – 'The Cat Crept In', 'Lonely This Christmas', 'Oh Boy' – continued and they began buying the odd trapping of wealth – Dave bought a Pontiac car with the number plate MUD 401 – they would still bend over to help you get your story or photo. There was never a tantrum, a sulk, a sarky word from the boys – kind of like the UK Osmonds, but without the religion.

Doing their life story entailed visits to their own patch of London – the Mitcham area of Surrey. The boys had more or less grown up together – no one could accuse them of being a 'manufactured' group – and one or other of them had been playing together in bands since their teens. It was fun to visit their modest little terrace and semi-detached homes – most of them, bar guitarist Ray Stiles who was married, still lived with Mum and Dad. Rob, the quietest, shyest one of the band, still had his soft toy collection in his little bedroom at Hackbridge.

We went to their old schools, the shops they used to visit for guitar strings, the patch of green where they used to play football, and to St Mark's Church Hall where they played their first-ever gig, and then to the local pub to sit over a few drinks.

Seeing their background and hearing about some of the early jobs they had before turning pro – Les Gray had been a messenger in an advertising agency, Dave an apprentice electrical fitter, Rob Davis a wages clerk – I realised why I liked their company so much. They really were working class lads who got lucky – albeit with some talent to help them along – and just carried on and on feeling great about life because wasn't pop the best thing, didn't it just beat 9 to 5 at the factory and earning a tenner a week? Mud played pop because they loved the whole business, I wrote about it because I loved it. We were all escapees from a life that could have been so much worse – and that was why we all got on so well.

Ronnie Scott's Soho club was still one of the main venues we'd arrive at if we wanted some fun, and it was still playing host to the best press receptions in town.

In June we saw a guy called Ed Welch at Ronnie's. Ed was a talented songwriter and keyboard player who had released an album called *Clowns* back in 1973, which was one of my all-time favourite LPs. He'd signed my copy for me at his first press reception and he was another of those people you just get on with.

Unfortunately he just didn't have the right pushiness or aplomb or look to make it as a chart star but his musical talents and his knack of getting along with everyone were ensuring that he was never out of work. We met up several times in the early '70s but the one I remember best was a boozy lunch in the upstairs room at the Henekey's pub in Kingly Street, at the back of Regent Street. I'm not sure how we all ended up there – I've a feeling we'd been to a late morning reception in the area (it could even have been yet another one for Welch himself) and had then decided we were all ravenous – but anyway there was Nigel Hunter, Rodney Burbeck, Ed Welch, a couple of others, me – and Spike Milligan.

Just off the Bayswater Road, near where my sister lives, there is a posh block called Orme Square. When I come up from Oxford to visit her at her small flat in Talbot Road, we sometimes walk up Hereford Road, past Orme Square and over the traffic lights into Hyde Park via Black Lion Gate.

'Do you know who lives there?' she asks me, pointing at the huge terraces of Orme Square. 'Spike Milligan!'

'How do you know that?'

'Oh, everyone knows. He spends a lot of time in the park, near the kiddies' playground. I think he's restoring the carved elves, and things!'

And we walk over to where she's talking about and there he is. And one minute he's smiling and nice and joking with the dozen or so people who are watching him. And next minute he's shouting and telling us we're ruining his work, his concentration. We're all bastards and what are we doing here anyway? Why don't we go away?

So we do.

Today at lunch we're all laughing and joking and Spike is telling stories then Ed's telling stories and it's a wonderful lunch. And I look at Spike and I remember, back at home in our semi down the Middleton Cheney Road, Banbury, in the '50s, my brother Rob was the biggest Goons fan in the world. Every week he tuned in to them and we'd listen. I didn't get the humour myself, but I was only about 7.

If my brother could see me here today, having lunch with Spike Milligan, he'd go wild! Wait till I tell him … So I sit there and do my best to chat to Spike but all the while I'm thinking … go carefully, be careful …. he could just turn.

I found out later that Ed and Spike were to begin collaboration on an album called *The Snow Goose*, based on the book of the same name by Paul Gallico, and that's why Ed had brought Spike along for lunch. The album, recorded by the London Symphony Orchestra, was eventually released in 1976, and after that Spike and Ed worked together at least once more.

Though I'd been to the States in 1973 for a week with the reader Judi, that visit had been so short and so focused on giving her a good time, and we packed so much in, that I hadn't really had what I thought of as a proper USA experience. So when Betty suggested that I should fly over for two weeks in July, and combine filing stories in LA with a week or so with The Osmonds in Vegas and in their home town of Provo in Utah, I was more than happy to agree. By this time I had been abroad so many times, for work and for private holidays, that travelling around on my own held no fear.

In fact, my long-term problems with feelings of inferiority, always wanting to please, never being able to say no or stick up for myself and worrying myself into a frazzle about the most basic of interviews or meetings had, I realised, just about all faded away. I was beginning, at last, to feel happy in my own skin and to have the inner confidence that, apparently, I had always appeared to have on the outside.

So I got organised, packed plenty including a bikini or two, and left Heathrow for LA on July 21st. Once again, Cyril met me at the airport and we headed to my hotel, the Holiday Inn, Wilshire Boulevard. I was coming up in the world! This was a bit better than the manky old Roosevelt and the area was much, much better. This was much more like the America of my young teenage dreams – modern, sleek, dynamic.

Okay, nowadays the Holiday Inn is synonymous with bargain basement naff, but in those days it was swish.

I was on my own, and Cyril was on his own, so our intention was to have ourselves a good time for the first four days in LA. With the help of our reporter in LA, Janey Milstead, he had set up for me a few interviews with 'ordinary' LA teens, so one day we headed south for miles and miles and miles – God how sprawling and boring South LA was – and eventually arrived about two hours late at a rather basic and dilapidated hut of a house where the 'typical teen' lived, and she gave us a run down, and a series of photos, all about her life and times. At the end of it, I realised that all those years ago when I dreamed of living the American dream, in truth, I had been much, much, better off where I was.

Another day we headed up the coast through Santa Monica to Malibu beach where we photographed a girl who more closely matched my long-ago idea of what a Californian girl might look like, and how she might spend her time. She surfed a little, sunbathed a lot and had the blonde hair and good figure. But I still found the lifestyle depressing and I couldn't really figure out why except that it was all, somehow, a bit pointless.

Back in LA, though, Cyril knocked himself out to show me the bits of the city that he enjoyed – so we went clubbing on Hollywood Boulevard, dined at Benihana, had supper with some friends of his in West Hollywood, and drove up into the hills one night to dine at a 'typical British pub' – not very good but the view was fantastic. To stand there, finally, and see for myself all the lights of LA stretched out for miles, and then the Pacific Ocean – it was worth coming all that way just for that.

I was due to fly out to Las Vegas next – but Cyril had a better idea.

'What do you want to fly for?'

'Well, I'm booked.'

'I'm driving over – why don't you come with me? It's a great drive – I'll cancel your ticket.'

Not being a huge fan of driving long distances, I wasn't sure about this but didn't want to hurt his feelings after he'd given me a great few days, so I agreed, thank goodness.

We set off very early in the morning so that we could get quite a long way before the temperature in the Mojave Desert, which we had to cross, got too hot.

We drove through all the suburbs of LA that I only knew via song titles – Pasadena, San Bernadino, and so on. Before we'd even got out of that city, I was excited. We drove east as the sun rose towards us, and within an hour we were cruising just within the speed limit along highway Interstate 15 with gigantic vistas of deserts, flat-top mountains, cacti and sands every way you looked. It was phenomenal. I was speechless. It was the best thing.

'See up to the left?' said Cyril as we passed a town called Barstow – 'that's Death Valley. Pity we haven't got time to go up there!'

Now how many movies have you seen, the old Westerns, with Death Valley in them? Cyril was giving me my own personal ride though every one of my dreams and it just couldn't have been better.

In Vegas we checked into the Tropicana again, and an hour or two later we were with The Osmonds, who were doing three weeks of cabaret in the same hotel. By now worldwide Osmondmania was such that Vegas was overrun with fans intent on seeking out Donny and the brothers.

The family had suites at the hotel, which made my working life great. First, I had to file the LA stories and photos– in those days you had no email, no internet, no fax even … I took along the smallest portable typewriter you could get in those days, quite a heavyweight thing lent to me by Betty, plus typing paper and envelopes, and literally typed out my stories in the hotel rooms, then Cyril would add his rolls of film to my bits of paper and we'd drive to the airport to send them off back to the UK by courier.

But once I'd filed the backlog of copy, I had two hours to myself every morning before I would have to get ready and see one or other of the Osmonds for yet more stories and pics to fill the *Osmonds' World* magazine and the pages of *Fab*.

By this time I had got the hang of sunbathing. For years I had been a pale-skinned, blue-eyed redhead and every time I had tried to sunbathe I had burnt or not changed colour at all. I'd also been put off sunbathing, and indeed, heat, by Veronica Hill.

We're lying on towels in the back garden and she's covered in olive oil and she's already as brown as brown. God how I hate lying next to her, it makes my own skin look awful. I look like a ghost, a pink-tinged ghost. And I'm roasting and sweating and I'm bored, and she's said I've got to stay here until she says I can get up and go. So I do.

And next day, as the heatwave continues, she makes me get on the bus with her into Oxford and then she makes me take off my shoes and walk barefoot on the pavements, which are so hot I can hardly bear to put even a toe on the ground, let alone take my whole weight on my thin, bare, pink-skinned soles. But she makes me. And she laughs. And she calls me a baby for minding.

Back home my feet are burnt so badly I can't put my shoes on, or even walk, the next day. Mum isn't too pleased. Mrs Hill can't believe her daughter would do such a thing. I must be lying, she says. And Mum's too frightened of annoying Mrs Hill to disagree too long or too loud.

I eventually found out that if I sunbathed very, very gradually, just a little bit at a time building up, just like they tell you in all the sensible beauty articles every summer, then I could produce a pleasant, light tan. And I couldn't wait to try out how much of a tan I could get without burning during my time in Vegas. So I would get up early every morning, put on my bikini, tie my hair up, put on my robe, my sandals, my sunglasses, my hat and my sun cream, and head out of my room down through the gardens of the hotel to my favourite spot on a sunbed in a secluded corner. At this time – from around 8 to 9 a.m. every morning – there was hardly anyone about as people would stay up all night in the casinos or seeing shows or drinking; no one but a mad person would be sunbathing this early. And that was me.

Eventually I had such a nice tan I could have cried with joy. So *there*, Veronica Hill – so *there*! The bikini marks didn't look so good – no way was topless sunbathing an option then and in that place – but you can't have everything.

As soon as the days began to get really hot, I was indoors, showering and changing to do my work with the family. Alan Osmond had just married his girlfriend Suzanne so everyone was bubbling – it was a good week. By this time we all got along very well, and the members of the family seemed to forget I was there, at least some of the time, which, from my point of view, was ideal.

By this time I had stopped attempting to get underneath 'the façade' and down to the 'real' Osmonds. Either they were superbly controlled actors – which conjures up the scenario that every time I left the room for the day, within seconds they'd all be letting out their breath, and would be cussing and swearing, breaking open the brandy, hitting each other and generally being the other-planet Osmonds. Or they were genuinely whiter than white people who truly believed in their faith, their morals and really did feel that it was of the utmost importance to be nice to their fellow man, no matter who.

I had to believe the latter was true. I didn't think it would have been possible to maintain a front for every single one of the hundreds of people they met every week of their lives. And no dark stories about them ever came out in the press at all – it wasn't until many years later, when some of the Osmonds themselves began to admit that everything hadn't always been exactly perfect, and they hadn't always enjoyed every minute of that mad life of theirs, that you could read anything other than corn about the boys and the whole family.

Anyway, whatever – I had grown to like each one of them very much, and to respect them and their beliefs. I certainly respected their work ethic, their professionalism and their ability to work as a team, and have a laugh as well. Before most shows, they would line up backstage and do some rehearsal, rather than sit around and chat or read or watch TV. I found this rehearsal time more fascinating than the actual shows – five tall, strong, young men practising dance moves to 'Crazy Horses' on a wooden floor, making a beat, singing, with all the intensity of a battalion getting ready for war. It was like the whole room might explode any minute but it was also a bit like the Indians are waiting to attack just behind that horizon over there. You can hear a drumbeat or a rhythmic noise and you're not sure what's going to happen next. It got the adrenalin going, anyway.

In the evenings Cyril and I walked downtown and I would almost literally walk into lamposts, people and cars because my head was swivelling in every direction trying to take it all in. You look at photos of '70s Vegas now and it looks like a little hick town – but at the time, it seemed wondrous in its glamour, glitter, tackiness and sheer American pizazz.

The one thing I didn't do was place one bet in any of the casinos. I don't like to bet. I was maybe the only person ever who spent a week in Las Vegas and wasn't even tempted to part with a nickel for a fruit machine. That is, of course, apart from The Osmonds themselves.

Dad has stolen all my brother's savings. My brother Rob is 19, ten years older than me and he had been working at the local cinema and gradually he managed to save £100; he told us over Sunday lunch, and I'd never seen him so proud. And now he has been called up into the Air Force for his National Service, and Dad has forged his signature on his Post Office book, and stolen the money. Turns out Dad has been borrowing money from Mother's friends the Williams, and mother has found out, and Dad stole the money to pay off the Williams, and has admitted that he has run up debts gambling. No one will tell me anything, I just found all this out by keeping my ears open. If you're quiet, people will say things and they don't remember you're there.

So now Mum's in the Ashurst Clinic (with depression – no one told me but I heard), Dad and Rob are fighting in the kitchen and there's a knife and my Dad's face is bleeding, and I run across the garden to Mrs Licorice the neighbour and she comes and shouts at them and stops them fighting and Rob leaves home. He never comes back again.

I'm nearly 11 and things aren't a lot better. Now my older sister Ann is leaving home, too; she's living at a hotel in Banbury where she has a waiting job while she finishes at college. And when Mum comes back from another spell in the clinic we're leaving home as well, and I have to go and stay with Gran in Buckingham for a few weeks and go to the Latin School there, while Mum finds us somewhere to live. I bet it is going to be with Mrs Hill.

And I'm right; a few weeks later Mum and I move into the house in Eynsham with Mrs Hill, Veronica Hill, Clive Hill and Richard Hill. And we stay there for a year or two until we all move to Botley.

The outdoor thermometer showed 110°F; I wilted, but I survived. It was dry desert heat. On 31 July Cyril drove me to the airport and I caught the short flight to Salt Lake City where one of the guys from The Osmonds' office met me and took me to stay at a motel – a come down, to say the least, as it barely had a restaurant – round the corner from the Osmonds' home, the Riviera Apartments in a small town called Provo.

Most of the family were still in Vegas, but Mother had come back, along with Jimmy and Marie. We had two days, during which time Olive Osmond showed me everything she could show me at that apartment block – a very modest home indeed for such a famous family. I had the grand tour of Jimmy's bedroom with his bunk bed and trapdoor, Marie's bedroom, Donny's bedroom, the other bedrooms, the small music room and studio in the basement, the kitchen, the sitting room – and that was about it.

I had the tour of Salt Lake City – clean. The tour of Brigham Young University where a couple of the boys had done a short spell of studying or played sports. The trip to look at the salt lake flats – boring.

One of the Osmond helpers drove me up to Sundance, the new ski area that had been bought five years earlier by Robert Redford, partly as a conservation project. There was little to see as, ahead of his time, he didn't want skyscraper hotels and casinos – he wanted wooden lodges and minimal fuss. The original eco-resort. But we did manage to see the man himself – walking across towards the wood-clad reception building, he gave us a wave. Then he seemed to decide that he would come over – the place wasn't exactly packed with people – and say Hi. And that was how I came to meet, briefly, one of the most famous movie stars of the day, at home in his own surroundings. To be honest, he wasn't much to swoon over in real life – quite short, quite poor skin – but I was glad to have seen him.

Apart from these few jaunts out, a lot of the time I was in Utah Olive and I would sit at the Riviera Apartments with a glass of orange juice or root beer, while she told me tales of the early days, and tried to explain their faith to me. She'd also give me recipes – she was an avid cook and would bottle and store and freeze and dry foods and loved to bake. For all their healthy ways – no alcohol, smoking, caffeine, plenty of exercise and a clean lifestyle, Olive was extremely overweight and I think the baking might have had something to do with it.

On Friday 2 August I flew to LA and caught my return plane to London.

The rest of the year seemed pretty dull after that. I journeyed down to Barnes in south-west London to visit Alan Price at his home on a boiling hot summer day. I'd been looking forward to this as The Animals had been one of my favourite bands in my teens. He was at home on his own, a small, enthusiastic, motivating kind of person. He had just compiled a tape for his wife – Wiff, he called her (or was it whiff?) – of her favourite music and played me some of it. He was in a great mood. Then we went out into his back garden where there was a quite large swimming pool.

And this was when things begin to go slightly wrong.

'Why don't you have a swim, Judy?' Alan said.

Now you may remember, from my Tunisian escapade, that I wasn't much of a swimmer, and the last thing on earth I wanted was to get in his pool. Yes, I was stiflingly hot. But even apart from the swimming consideration, there were other factors. I'd spent ages doing my hair and make-up in honour of Alan Price, and I didn't fancy getting it all ruined and having my straight hair turn all frizzy in front of him as it dried out. And of course, I hadn't got a cozzie.

'That's kind of you, Alan – but I haven't got a costume!'

'Oh – not to worry about that – there are lots of them in the changing room …' and Price pointed to a small wooden hut. 'Go on – off you go! It'll cool you down fantastic.'

By this time I was beginning to feel as hot and uncomfortable and embarrassed as I used to in the early *Fab* days at the drop of any hat. But I held my ground.

'Look, Alan – I'm not a great swimmer and I've got to go soon. I think I'll give it a miss if you don't mind.'

I'd snubbed his hospitality and he showed me the door, politely but firmly, within minutes. And for years after I felt bad every time I thought about that – I should have shown willing and got in the damn pool. It wouldn't have killed me.

Later that year, I interviewed Kenny Jones of The Faces at the Portobello Hotel in Notting Hill, TV presenter Leslie

Crowther at home in Twickenham (during which he explained to me at length his love for collecting pot lids) and Rod Stewart at the Kensington Gardens Hotel. All I remember about that interview with Rod was that he arrived in a dapper brown tweed suit (this, you will remember, was the Rod era of glam rock and the spikey hairdo and platform shoes) and for explanation told me that he had decided to dress to suit the seasons – as it was autumn he was wearing autumn colours, in winter he might wear white, in spring yellow … and so on. Whether he stuck to that I don't know, but I don't think so.

The Boss and I, surprisingly enough still together despite almost everyone we knew having secretly placed bets on how many weeks it would last, spent Christmas at Cathcart Road. We bought a tree and decorated it and on Christmas Eve invited Wyn and Gerry (they of the Frankie Howard lunch) round to go out for a meal at the bistro in Hollywood Road. They had just bought a kitten and for some reason brought it round and left it in the flat while we went out for the meal. When we got home, the kitten had knocked the tree over and eaten most of the glass decorations – but by some miracle, was still alive.

'Waddayaknow?' said Wyn (who was an ex-New York police department chief) 'the puddy ate the pine'.

We'd had too much to drink to worry about the kitten but next time they came round they left it at home. Well, either that, or it died; they never said.

It was a pretty good Christmas, anyway.

By early 1975, Betty Hale deemed that Slade were now legendary enough that I was to do their life story in *Fab*. This entailed spending several sessions with them and as ever they were good fun.

I was still doing the Dream Come True features most of the time and when I received one from two 13 year olds who wanted to go pony trekking, I decided this one was too good to pass by. I had been a typical pony-mad child and teenager and had only stopped riding when I moved to London from the country. But having met Karen Gill through the David Essex Dream Come True, who was a keen rider, The Boss and I had begun driving down to Epsom, where she lived, to ride at a stables there every Saturday. The Boss had never ridden before in his life but the force of my persuasive powers made him give it a go despite the fact that he couldn't understand how you could steer without a wheel.

Anyway, it had re-ignited my love for riding so I quite fancied a couple of days somewhere pony trekking. Sue James, the fashion editor, knew someone who had just returned from a place in South Wales which she said was good. I booked it up for April and five of us – the two girls, the photographer David Porter and his wife Clarissa, and me, drove down to the Half Moon Inn in the Llanthony valley in the heart of the Black Mountains, and spent two wet days trekking around the hills.

I was amazed to find somewhere so remote and beautiful so near to England. Plus, the Inn was good fun and the people who ran the trekking centre – a busty blonde woman called Janice who would ride around the muddy slopes on a Welsh pony in full hunting gear, and the local farmer called Trevor, were truly mad in the nicest sense. When I got back to London, I suggested to The Boss that we should book our own weekend there later in the spring.

So in May we arrived at the Half Moon. This time the weather was gorgeous and the first two days of our break were splendid – The Boss's horse was called Killer and on the first day he learnt to jump logs and had a great time. The first night, after an evening in the Inn's cosy bar, Trevor and Janice invited us to go poaching for trout by torchlight in the River Olchon. And so we did, that very minute; probably a mistake in high heels but at least I can say I have been a poacher and not that many people can say that.

Next day, The Boss, overconfident after day one, and nursing a hangover, fell off his horse up the mountain and got concussion, so we had to skip the last day's trekking. Instead, we drove north through the narrow mountain pass until at the road's highest point an amazing view – not quite on the Mojave Desert scale, but impressive nevertheless – lay in front of us. We stopped the car and got out and it was my first view of Wales proper.

A few miles further on was a little town called Hay-on-Wye, straddling the English/Welsh border, and here we stopped for lunch and a walk around. It was like stepping back in time, with ponies and cattle being driven through the streets to its bustling market.

In the window of the local estate agent was a pretty cottage, 2 miles from Hay. For something to do, we went to look at it. We'd been contemplating buying a terraced house in Fulham with the little money we had managed to save since we had been together – that is, what hadn't gone on booze, holidays and fancy vintage cars (for him) and taxis and clothes (for me).

To get to Yew Tree Cottage you had to go over a ford and down a track that ended in a bridle path. The little stone house was perched on a flat rock above a mountain stream, with a small garden and paddock area, surrounded by hills. Well, we never did buy the property in Fulham. We'd kind of fallen in love. We made an offer, we had it accepted, and that was how, in May 1975, I handed in my notice to *Fab*. I was to leave on 6 June after eight years.

I could have stayed on, as we were going to keep the Cathcart Road flat and just use the cottage for weekends. But The Boss had been badgering me for a year or two to leave – 'you're getting too old to be doing pop for a teen magazine'.

Until recently, I had totally disagreed with him – I was still having fun and could do the job without any worry or stress, I was reasonably paid and had several moonlighting jobs to boost the income and make a change – so why leave? But in the past few months I had begun to realise that perhaps it *was* time for a career move. I felt I might be able to go freelance.

I felt strangely nervous of going in to Betty's office to do the deed, once I'd made up my mind. I'd never handed in my notice before except from a Saturday job I'd had for six weeks in Oxford when I was 16, working in a clothing warehouse to save up enough money to go to Great Yarmouth for the weekend to see Billy Fury with my college friend Jenny.

'I wanted to see you because I've decided it's about time I left, Betty.'

'Well, I guessed as much. I'll be sorry to lose you, but I do agree with you – it's time you spread your wings a bit. How long have you been here?'

'Eight years, believe it or not!'

She began to smile and after a few seconds she said, 'Neither you nor I ever dreamt you'd be here that long, did we? You were nearly sacked so many times … but there was something about you. I did have faith in you. And I was right, you see.'

'Thank you Betty – and I'm sorry I made your life hell for a while. I could never work out if I wanted to be very good, or very bad. So I tried a bit of both. I thank Unity and you, you gave me the courage to be bad when I wanted to.'

In truth, I think Betty was like a parent – she helped to guide me through a displaced adolescence when I was not only naïve and stupid and over-trusting of people, but also seeing how far I could push her. She had tried all the things that parents do, including giving advice as necessary, being reasonable and forgiving, and then if that didn't work, bringing on the tough love.

Well now I was grown up, her work on shaping me was done, and it was time to go.

The only thing Betty and I never talked about was my home life – in particular, my relationship with The Boss. Having warned me off him all those years ago, I guess she felt it was an area best ignored.

Once I'd seen Betty and handed in my notice, I panicked, of course. But I had work lined up – *Osmonds' World* was still going strong and I had offers of regular freelance from

Record Mirror and *Woman* magazine. I was also going to write a TV column in *Fab* and become their new agony auntie. I had also, bizarrely, been asked by Tony Hatch – the original Simon Cowell-type mean judge on the top TV talent show of the '70s, *New Faces*, and one of the most successful songwriters of the day – to ghost-write his new 'how to make it in the music business' column for a monthly magazine. So I wasn't quite going to be taking my vows or queuing up at the dole office.

Halfway through my month's notice I was to spend my last block of time with The Osmonds. They arrived in London to do concerts and promotion and every day I would take a taxi to the large terraced house they had rented in Eaton Square, at the back of Knightsbridge, to see them. As it turned out, I wouldn't set eyes on any of them again for over thirty years. If I'd known, I might have even had a little cry.

I had one last freebie jaunt before my leaving party – a day at the Derby on 4 June. One of the PR companies had organised an old London bus to take a bunch of journalists and various pop stars and bands down to Epsom. David Porter and I were picked up along the route and on the bus, I was pleased to see, were all the Mud boys. They gave me a grand send-off with free Derby Day champagne and cake and I got so tipsy and maudlin that I sobbed all the way home.

Two days later I was given my leaving card and I was out of there. It had been a good blag. But it was time to go and grow vegetables, rediscover my inner country bumpkin, be Tony Hatch, and see what else life had to offer.

Epilogue

Some Time Later ...

So now fast forward. I'm on the train heading to Cardiff, Wales. It's nearly thirty-one years since my last day at *Fab* magazine and it's thirty-one years since I saw the people I'm on my way to visit. I'm looking forward to it.

The last time I heard from them was in October 1975, when I was in the intensive care unit, Princess Margaret Hospital, Swindon, after a car crash on the M4. They sent me a large bouquet of flowers and a telegram. In the years after my recovery, I moved on to other things, their star waned for a decade or two, and we lost touch.

I'm clutching a few tatty old photos of them and me, and of them taken by me, to jog their memories about the times we spent together. I expect they'll need it.

And now I'm in the foyer of St David's Hall, waiting for their PR, Jackie, to come and find me and take me backstage. It's amazing – these boys have a huge crowd of fans arriving at the hall, chanting and singing. Not quite like the old days

– then they were screaming teenagers, now a lot of them are middle-aged with a few extra pounds round their middles – just like the guys they're shouting for.

Now I'm backstage. And here they are – Merrill, Wayne, Jay and 'little' Jimmy Osmond – the Osmond Brothers, hugging me and greeting me and we're all laughing and of course we all remember each other and of course after a few minutes in each others' company the wrinkles and those extra pounds and the grey hairs fade away and we're young again.

I show them that old Book of Mormon given to me by their mother, Olive, during my US visit in 1973 and signed by all the family except Jimmy. He puts that right – he autographs it three decades late. And we have the obligatory backstage photo taken.

I could have chosen to seek out one of the many other icons of the '70s who are still working and still popular today, to round off this tale. But I chose The Osmonds – just because they sum up my '70s rather well.

I watch them perform, and when they strike up with 'Crazy Horses', a ghost of that old, pit-of-the-stomach feeling I used to have touches me. I remember what it was all about.

As Joni Mitchell once sang – give or take the odd word – you don't always appreciate what you've got till it's gone. We did pave paradise and put up a parking lot.

It wasn't all good. It was by no means all good.

But it wasn't half bad, was it?

Appendix

And What Happened to the Cast ...

◈ *Fab 208* magazine, with Betty Hale still
    editor, folded in 1981 after an admirable
    run of eighteen years. Betty celebrated her
    80th birthday in 2007 – and we shared a
    'fab' lunch in the Oxo Tower, London in
    December of that year.
◈ Unity Hall continued writing novels and
    biographies until her death in the early '90s.
◈ Billy Fury's 1969 marriage to Judith Hall
    broke up a few years later. Fury sent his
    friend Keith Moon to collect his luggage
    from the marital home. Fury went into semi-
    retirement in the late '70s and early '80s due
    to poor health, and shared a farmhouse in

Wales with his partner Lisa Rosen. He died on 28 January 1983 aged just 42.

◈ Jason Eddie lived in Liverpool until his death in September 2011 after several years of poor health. We were in touch again by email in recent years and made our peace.

◈ George of Edison Lighthouse died in the early '80s. Two of the band, Stuart Edwards and Dave Taylor, were still performing as an Edison Lighthouse duo as recently as 2003.

◈ Hal Carter went on to build up one of the biggest music management businesses in London – the Hal Carter Organisation, specialising in '60s and '70s artistes. Hal died in July 2004 aged 69 and his daughter Abbie took over the business.

◈ Jimmy Campbell, despite his seminal album *Son of Anastasia* (1969), never achieved huge fame at the time, and died in 2007, but his old material is now recognised for its brilliance.

◈ Biba moved to the old Derry and Toms Kensington department store in 1973 but was never the same, and it closed in the mid-'70s. The Biba name was revived in 2006 as a new fashion collection.

◈ Tony Prince left Luxy to start up the DJ bible, *MixMag* and the international Disco Mix Club or DMC, the world's leading company, label, magazine and website for DJ culture. He lives in Buckinghamshire.

◈ The Osmonds' fantastic popularity worldwide began to fade after the mid-'70s until reviving during the pop nostalgia wave since the millennium. Most of the brothers spent the '80s and '90s struggling to support their growing families and coping with near-bankruptcy. Merrill suffered from depression and diabetes, Wayne a brain tumour, Alan has multiple sclerosis, and in 2004 Jimmy suffered a stroke. The brothers now have over 50 children and grandchildren between them and in 2017 will celebrate sixty years in show business.

◈ Donny Osmond went on to a solo career starring in *Joseph and his Amazing Technicolour Dreamcoat* on stage for several years in the '90s. Now he performs and tours once more with sister Marie.

◈ Olive Osmond died, aged 79, two years after suffering a massive stroke, in May 2004.

◈ George Osmond died in 2007.

◈ Keith Moon died on 7 September 1978 of an overdose of Heminevrin, pills prescribed to help him overcome his alcohol addiction.

◈ Jim Morrison died in Paris on 3 July 1971, of heart failure brought on by heavy drinking.

◈ Richard Harris died of cancer, aged 72, on 25 October 2002.

◈ Peter Wyngarde was caught up in a homosexual scandal later in the '70s and his career never recovered.

◈ 'Six foot of dick' morphed into Richard Girling, highly-respected investigative journalist for *The Sunday Times* and campaigning author.

◈ Richard Chamberlain has sustained a career in films and TV ever since *Dr Kildare* and finally came out as gay in 2003, saying he'd been too frightened to mention it before.

◈ David 'Kid' Jensen became one of the UK's most popular radio DJs on BBC Radio 1 and then on Capital Gold. He is now a freelance radio presenter and lives in Surrey with wife Gudrun. He has three children and, last time I heard, two grandchildren.

◈ Dave Cash is still DJing for BBC local radio and we are still in touch. He would like to point out that the car he used to drive around London in was not a Jaguar but an Aston Martin DB5.

◈ Tony Blackburn moved back to the BBC, after a sixteen-year absence, in 2004, as a BBC Radio London presenter; he also works for Radio 2 and is a regular in many TV programmes.

◈ I last saw Nigel Hunter back in 2007 when he came to the lunch with Betty Hale at the Oxo Tower.

◈ Rodney Burbeck is still a busy media professional and owner of Rodney Burbeck Publishing Services.

◈ Julie Webb got married, moved to Rutland, had five children and became a reporter on a local newspaper.

◈ Sadly Georgina Mells and I lost touch many years ago but I have heard she lives in her parents' old house in Buckinghamshire.

◈ Jim Dale MBE, 80, lives in the USA. He is a highly respected actor who is in the American Theatre Hall of Fame, and performed his one-man show *Just Jim Dale* in London's West End in 2015 to mark fifty years as a theatre performer.

◈ Roy Carr continued as a music journalist and broadcaster, became an author and record producer, and is still a much-respected authority of the music of the era. His Facebook page says he lives in Yokohama, Bolivia.

◈ Noel Edmonds was banished to the BBC wilderness in 1999 after many years as one of the UK's top entertainment presenters – but made an amazing comeback with Channel 4's *Deal or No Deal*.

◈ John Alderton is still with Pauline Collins.

◈ Gene Pitney died in April 2006 after a gig in Cardiff. The year before, my brother Rob saw the 'wailing tom cat' perform at Llandudno in 2005 – and said he was brilliant.

◈ Leonard Nimoy continued to act into the '90s but announced his retirement from movies in 2002 and became a photographer and poet. He died in February 2015 at the age of 83. Nimoy's last tweet before he died said, 'A life is like a garden. Perfect moments can be had, but not preserved, except in memory. LLAP*.'
* Live Long and Prosper – Mr Spock's most famous catchphrase.

◈ Jack Wild died of alcohol and smoking-related mouth cancer on 1 March 2006.

◈ Richard Beckinsale's baby Kate grew up to be the Hollywood film star Kate Beckinsale.

◈ Richard Beckinsale died of a heart attack in March 1979 aged 31.

◈ I have no idea what happened to Mrs Hill and her children and I haven't got the heart to find out.

◈ Adam Faith died of a heart attack at 62 in 2003 shortly after coming off stage while acting in a play in the Midlands. His daughter Katya is a film producer and cameraman.

- ◈ PJ Proby is 77 and lives in England. In 1977 he played Elvis on the West End stage, now has a thriving fan club and appears in concert and in revival tours around the UK as well as running his own recording label.
- ◈ George Best died in November 2005 of complications from treatments for alcoholism.
- ◈ Babs Lord went on to marry actor Robert Powell and became a world class sailor.
- ◈ Les Gray of Mud died of a heart attack in Portugal in February 2004.
- ◈ Dave Mount of Mud left the music business and worked in insurance until his death in December 2006 aged 57.
- ◈ Ray Stiles and Rob Davis of Mud got together for the first time in many years to do some gigs in autumn 2015. Ray had been playing in The Hollies, while Rob had become a successful songwriter having co-written 'Can't Get You Out of My Head' for Kylie Minogue.
- ◈ My mother Enid died on 17 December 2006 aged 91.
- ◈ My father John died aged 75 in November 1982.
- ◈ Andy Williams died in September 2012 at the age of 84. He had a UK hit in 1999 with 'Music to Watch Girls By' and in recent years had his own Moon River Theatre in Branson, USA and he performed until 2009. I went along to

the Birmingham Symphony Hall in mid-2007 to see him in concert and he was still in good voice. I considered arriving at the stage door to hand him my IOU, but thought better of it.

◈ Gary Glitter was sent to jail in Thailand for sex offences against children, returned to the UK and is now serving a sixteen-year sentence for further historical offences.

◈ Tony Barrow lives in Lancashire and in 2005 wrote a biography of his time with The Beatles.

◈ Tony Brainsby died in March 2000.

◈ Spike Milligan died from liver failure in February 2002 .

◈ Ike Turner died in California in December 2007 aged 76.

◈ Ed Welch is a successful TV theme tune composer.

◈ Ronnie Scott's Club in Frith Street continues to be a popular jazz venue, and still plays host to private parties. Ronnie died in 1996 from an accidental overdose of sleeping pills and brandy.

◈ The Talk of the Town closed in the '80s and the building has had several re-incarnations. It is now the Hippodrome Casino.

◈ The Finsbury Park Rainbow (Astoria) was left to rot for several years but has been restored, is a listed building and now a Pentecostal church.

◈ Rules restaurant was sold by John Wood and his wife Pamela in 1984 and Buck's Bar was demolished to make room for extra tables. Buck Taylor died of cancer in the late '70s.

◈ Julia Morley is still chairman of the Miss World competition – and the swimsuit round has now been abandoned.

◈ David Cassidy, and many stars of the '60s and '70s, including David Essex OBE, Suzi Quatro and Slade do regular revival tours in the UK and abroad.

◈ David Bowie died on 10 January 2016 at the age of 69. RIP 'the new boy from Kent'. You did OK.

◈ And me? My freelance career as a writer began with showbiz interviews and 'human interest' features for many publications including *The Daily Mail* and *Woman*, as well as *Fab* and the music press. Continuing in the random fashion that much of my working life had followed, in my late 20s I was offered a job as editor of a national slimming magazine which, for reasons that escape me now, I accepted. The Boss and I moved full-time to a house not far from our little weekend cottage, and so began a new life raising children, bossing freelance contributors around (and finding out what

Betty Hale had to put up with), writing books, and growing those veg. I still live in that same house in the countryside on the Welsh Borders near Hay-on-Wye. The Boss (whose name is, in fact, Tony) and I married in April 1980 and we went on to have two sons – Will who is a burgeoning music scene photographer and senior carer with the charity Scope, and Chris who is a father, musician, DJ/producer, has performed at Glastonbury and – funnily enough – is a vegetable grower extraordinaire. Rock on!

Acknowledgements

I would like to thank:

♪ My sister Ann McDonnell without whom my *Fab* days would never have begun, and of course Unity Hall who was brave enough to give me the job.

♪ Betty Hale, my 'third parent', without whom the book would have been considerably shorter, as would my career.

♪ Jane Turnbull for her support, time and encouragement.

♪ All the team at The History Press who have done such a brilliant job on producing this edition of the book.

♪ Tony Prince, Chris Charlesworth, Abbie
   Carter, Nigel Hunter and Annie Moore for
   help with facts, names, dates and details.

♪ Jackie Skinner for her help in arranging a
   latter day meet up with the Osmonds.

♪ Jimmy and all the Osmonds for finding
   time in a hectic schedule to meet and
   reminisce.

♪ All the *Fab* photographers, some of
   whose photos may appear in this book –
   with special thanks to Peter Pugh-Cook,
   Roger Brown, Roger Morton and David
   Porter.

♪ Everyone who took time to read the
   manuscript and pass comment on it.

♪ Most of the colleagues I met along the
   way who enriched those years, including
   several of those already mentioned
   above, as well as David ('no longer a
   Kid') Jensen, Rodney Burbeck, Roy Carr,
   Gordon Coxhill, and the many 'residents'
   of the Hoop and Grapes and Rules
   restaurant.

♪   Most of the entertainment, music, film, TV and show business stars and would-be stars I met during the years, for providing such a rich source of memories. With special mention to Mr Spock himself Leonard Nimoy, Andy Williams, Slade and Mud.

♪   The Boss, for obvious reasons.

♪   Everyone who was at *Fab* at the same time as I was – including Georgina Mells, Julie Webb (now Emberton), Sue Lumsden (now Hegarty), Tom, whose real name was Brian Thomas, Ann Wilson (now Annie Davison), Jackie Fearn (now Wyatt), Bev Ballard, Louette Harding, Sue James and David Porter – for making my years there such fun.

♪   And I would like to remember the friends, acquaintances and interviewees who have passed on but will never be forgotten and are, hopefully, having a great party somewhere: Billy Fury, Andy Williams, Leonard Nimoy, Hal Carter, Gene Pitney, Freddie Mercury, Les Gray, Dave Mount, Jim Morrison, Richard Beckinsale, Jason Eddie, Spike Milligan, The Beast – and – of course – Keith Moon.

Index